About This Girl
この女の子について

About This Girl
この女の子について

My path to success, womanhood,
love and so much more

Gemma Manning

I dedicate this book to all the amazing women in my life—my loving mother, Robbie, my big sister, Natalie, the strong women who came before me including my big *and* little nanny, and my daughters, Charlotte and Amelie.

Gemma 'Louise' as I affectionately call her, is a tough cookie. In fact, she's more than just a tough cookie. She's like one of those really resilient, hard-to-break, gobstopper things you had as a kid that just kept going and going, refusing to disappear; the ones that you knew would last forever, but would always put a big smile on your face every single time you had one.

That pretty much sums up this little pocket rocket in more ways than one—she's a prime example of a motivated, driven female making strides in this world whilst refusing to accept no for an answer, and refusing to let inequality stand in the way of what she believes in.

I first met Gemma in a baggage check-in line on the way to Antarctica of all places, and I knew that after spending some time with her in one of the remotest but breathtaking places in the world, that this little dancing queen was going places. It's been incredibly rewarding having seen what Gemma has achieved and I have no doubt there is so much more to come.

She has raised two incredibly beautiful, confident, and well-mannered girls, grown a business from a little office into a thriving international enterprise, and has partied with me many times at Sir Richard Branson's home, Necker Island.

This book is well worth a read for any aspiring entrepreneur, single mum, yet alone any female in business. It'll fill your heart with warmth, ambition, and happiness, and leave you smiling in every way—exactly like Gemma Louise does every time you see her.

Congratulations, Chicken.

Chris Dutton

Founder, *The CEO Magazine*

This book describes the inspirational journey of an amazing young woman, one who is always upbeat and optimistic in spite of the knocks, always encouraging of others, always supportive of those who need help. It's been a privilege to be able to observe Gemma's success, most notably in leading Australian business to the Asian opportunity. This is a great read, and a template for women (and men!) to follow.

Phil Forrest

Non-Executive Director

I first met Gemma when she was invited to Perth to speak at an Innovation summit. We shared the stage and I was immediately impressed by her vision, her clarity, her professionalism and her quiet confidence. Gemma had recently set up her business in Singapore, where I was born and had lived for 12 years, so I had a good understanding of the incredibly wise messages she was presenting. One of my immediate reactions was "Wow, that was gutsy setting up a business overseas in a new market". She certainly made a very strong first impression on me!

Gemma and I then met again when she decided to establish a business in Perth. Once again, I was struck by the boldness of her decision. Over a few meetings, Gemma talked about her exciting plans, as well as some of the challenges she was encountering, which resonated with me because my father had faced similar difficulties when he migrated to Western Australia and set up his own business in the 1960s. I was confident that Gemma would succeed because her plans were sound, she was focused and there was a deep determination in her eyes.

Having attended a number of Gemma's events and pitch sessions, I have to say I have been really impressed by the quality of the graduates from her courses. Perhaps the most notable was the pitch session by the Deaf and Hard of Hearing group—it was so heart-warming to see young people, who faced significant challenges in their lives, confidently presenting their cases, seeking support for their new enterprises.

And now Gemma, serial entrepreneur, businesswoman and mother, has found time to write a book—*About This Girl*. Amazing! What a remarkable testament to her energy, ability and resilience. Go Gemma—may you continue to inspire all those you meet along your journey.

Peter Klinken
Chief Scientist, Western Australia

Gemma Manning has written a captivating, compassionate and honest autobiography, a very real account of embracing change, dealing with life's curveballs and taking failure as a call to action. *About This Girl* is a true gift to anyone who has ever doubted themselves. It's a tale of courage and personal strength and is a beautiful example of the power of self-belief.

As a female leader and entrepreneur, in what remains a male dominated business world, Gemma has given a genuine account of the hardships which inequality brings, the wisdom and leadership traits needed to succeed, and the importance of finding your tribe.

I can't recommend it enough.

Oriel Morrison
Start-up Founder, Former international business news anchor

Gemma's book is a delightful read for those of us who want to know the lessons of resilience and grit on an entrepreneurial journey. Gemma authentically depicts the highs and lows she has experienced over many years and across multiple countries, which is sure to inspire and motivate anyone building their own business.

Luisa Wing
Founder and Author, Vermelho

There is no limit to what we, as women,

can accomplish.

— Michelle Obama

ISBN: 978-981-14-8069-0

DISCLAIMER
All the events in this memoir are true to the best of the
author's memory. Some names and identifying features
have been changed to protect the identity of certain parties.
The author in no way represents any company, corporation,
or brand, mentioned herein. The views expressed in this
memoir are solely those of the author.

Designed by Sarah and Schooling
Cover Illustration by Renee Pullen
Printed in Singapore

CONTENTS

FOREWORD

In May of 2016, I met Gemma on what can only be described as an experience of a lifetime. I had just hopped off a boat and into the back of a covered Jeep on Necker Island, Sir Richard Branson's private island. I remember my head was spinning as I took in all of the beauty of the island, tried to control my excitement for the week ahead, and also tried to remember the names of the other entrepreneurs I would be spending the week with. As fate would have it, I sat right next to Gemma in that Jeep. I remember immediately thinking how beautiful she was and immediately falling in love with her Aussie accent (she would say she loves my Southern accent too) as we swapped pleasantries and talked about our businesses and our families.

Over that week on Necker, Gemma and I shared stories of motherhood and entrepreneurship and the mess and the magic that come with balancing both of those. Little did we know it was the beginning of a strong friendship and bond that would span not only oceans, but years as well.

On my journey of starting and growing a business and becoming a mom to two while doing so (and also trying to be a great daughter, wife, sister, and friend), I have been truly blessed to have connections to those on my same path. I have also found tremendous value in the story of others who have gone before me. Those so-called "lonely" moments "at the top" aren't as lonely when you have a solid tribe around you. How blessed I am that Gemma is part of my tribe! Inspiring me and motivating me from the other side of the globe. And now *About This Girl* will do the same for so many more.

In 2019 I travelled to see Gemma in Singapore for a few days before a trip to China. On my last day there we met for coffee, which then turned into lunch, which then turned into window shopping and cocktails, which then turned into dinner. It was truly as if in the hours of that day we made up for the fact we hadn't met until we were in our mid-thirties. I left her that day a little sad that (due to my living in the US and she in Singapore) we would likely never be friends who could just pop over for a glass of wine on one of our porches, but also extremely grateful that I have her as a friend and that we live in a world where we can stay so connected virtually.

On that trip Gemma shared with me her work to help deaf and hard of hearing entrepreneurs and asked me to help teach her cohort. Helping deaf and hard of hearing individuals has been a passion of mine since childhood, as both of my parents have been deaf since infancy. It was another nod from the universe that we are held, we are guided; we must just be open to receiving. I think Gemma's story will show you more of the same.

Anything is possible. All the best life has to offer is here for us.

I have no doubt that this book will leave you inspired. That in that next moment for you of self-doubt or regret or despair, you may be able to call on a line or a page from this book and know you are not alone. Gemma has gone before you. She has and is paving the way for innovative thought, for taking the limits off yourself, and for leading with a compassionate heart and soul.

Ginger Jones, Founder and CEO of Jones Therapy
"Most Admired CEO", *Nashville Business Journal* 2019

Gemma, Ginger, Amelie and Charlotte
at PS Cafe in Singapore, 2019.

INTRODUCTION
ABOUT THIS GIRL

I'm trying to be myself more and more. The more
confidence you have in yourself... the more you realize
that this is you, and life isn't long. So get on with it!

— Kylie Minogue

There's nothing quite like a cutting remark to throw you off your game. One moment you're in your usual routine minding your own business, and the next you're thrown off it when someone says something so incredibly stupid you can't help but contemplate it.

It happened to me first thing in the morning, too. It was raining, so my daughter and I booked a Grab car. It stopped at her school and she got off to join the school run. I continued with the ride, indicating my office address as the final destination.

"So, where're you going?" the driver asked in what I'd assumed to be normal small talk.

"I'm going to my office."

"Oh? What do kind of work do you do?"

"I run my own marketing business."

I like being upfront with people, so I explained that I've a marketing company which I run out of Singapore. It's a business I'd started in Australia which has since branched out to the Asia-Pacific region. We service this region, so I've offices both here and in Australia.

"Oh... you must be *very* capable then."

He did not mean it as a compliment; there was nothing friendly in his reply, just plain condescension. Men, he continued, wouldn't find me attractive because I was "too strong and too capable."

I don't often stop to think about these things, but when a remark like that followed my explanation of a career which I'm very proud of, my stomach dropped and my blood turned to ice. I refused to engage thereafter and ignored his further attempts to chat. There was no point in getting into a fruitless argument, much less proving my worth to a stranger.

Dual incomes and women contributing to the household are expected in the modern world, but this driver still believed women can't be too intelligent—and weren't meant to be. On some level, he felt that such women were threatening to himself.

I would love to say that I got out of that Grab ride unfazed, simply laughing off that incident. But it had indeed upset me, because this was yet another occasion where someone had completely judged me because of my gender.

TOO THIS, NOT ENOUGH THAT

I know that my career is not the run of the mill, and when I talk about it, for some people it is unthinkable for a woman to be doing what I'm doing. Or worse, they downplay my efforts and professional expertise.

A few years ago, I was invited by the Western Australian government to speak at their state-wide innovation summit. My topic was on innovation, engagement and marketing in Asia, and the opportunities for Western Australia to promote itself as a strategic location in this area. In my presentation I spoke about entrepreneurship and made a small reference to my own entrepreneurial hero, Sir Richard Branson. I described very briefly that I'd met him, and that his story had inspired me to take even more risks with taking my business into Asia.

My entire presentation was focused on the journey of taking my business from Australia to Asia, and on the specific things that Western Australian companies should look for when they're entering Asia. But somehow, the emcee spent the rest of the event turning it into jabs at me for having met Branson. "Oh, but we all haven't had the chance to go meet Richard Branson, have we?" she would sneer. This time the remarks came from another woman, but they were no less condescending and demeaning to my work and my professionalism.

Running a business feels like climbing a mountain sometimes. The daily challenges often make me question why I keep at it. Why have I chosen this path—or why has this path chosen me? Am I too ambitious? Too driven? Am I simply plain crazy? Do I take on too much? Should I've taken an easier path? As rewarding as everything has been, the sacrifices have been just as painful.

But these fleeting doubts come and go. They prompt me to reflect on the day-to-day, and reaffirm the fact that success doesn't happen overnight. I started out in business with nothing. I've grown my business to where it is today from scratch; I didn't buy it from someone else, nor did I take it over. I've built it from the ground up and I've expanded it internationally, even won awards for my efforts. There is a lot of hard work to get to this point, on top of dealing with the gender issues that come when you're a woman in the world of business.

STORIES TO INSPIRE AND TEACH

I've always loved telling a story. When I was three years old, my mum and great-grandmother took me to the farmers' markets in Sydney and somehow, I managed to get myself lost in the crowds. Naturally worried, they enlisted the help of the local police to look for me. Where could a curious, fast-moving toddler have gone?

Eventually, they found me in a van that belonged to one of the stall owners. I was talking to some garden gnomes on sale, and I'd managed to somehow find my way there, crawling into the back of his van while he was none the wiser. I'd perched myself between the gnomes, and that was the scene that greeted them: me talking to an audience of gnomes, telling stories, and making introductions among my new friends.

I don't think we tell stories enough. I relate the first two incidents not to start this book off on a negative note, but to highlight the power of storytelling. Switch the names, locations and a couple of details around, and I'm sure you've had something similar happen to you too. Perhaps you've found your talents and efforts undermined because of gender stereotypes, because of physical abilities, your background, or any of the innumerable things that are completely out of your control. I believe that people can connect through stories, to know that there are others out there, going through similar journeys with similar pitfalls.

Having two daughters, I think it's important to share my story for them as well as other young girls and women around the world. This is also a story for men. Without me really thinking about it and setting out on this specific journey, I find myself now hoping that I'm making a difference for my girls' generation, by inspiring them to fly a bit higher by paving the way for them. If we don't raise our voices to talk about the good, the bad and the ugly, how are we going to set examples, and be those role models that future generations can look up to?

I did wonder why what the Grab driver had said affected me so much. I'm sure there are others for whom it would have just been water off a duck's back. But it did because I care—not just for myself, but for what his words mean for other women in my position. I'm sure he's far from the only person who holds those views.

When I'm passionate about something, I'm compelled to act. It doesn't feel right to be passionate about something and not act upon it. Acting on your convictions is part of living a purposeful life, and it is incredibly important for me to have a purpose. And with this book, I want my readers to understand that no one should have to deal with that sort of nonsense. No one should deal with the under handedness in business, just because we can say, it is just business. It is not good enough any longer. The tide needs to change, and it is in the hands of people who are inspired to change things for the better.

ABOUT THIS GIRL

I've titled this book loosely after an unreleased track from Kylie Minogue's 1997 album *Impossible Princess*. People who know me very well know how much I absolutely adore Kylie. Growing up, I was often told that I looked like her character, Charlene, from *Neighbours*, the soap opera she became popular through, because of the big hair and her petite figure.

I've always loved her music, and I still draw comfort and strength from her songs.

In fact, Kylie and her music have always been present in my life since I was an eight year old girl with the release of *Locomotion* and her first album, *Kylie Minogue*. I have been to almost all of her concerts in various cities, from Sydney and Brisbane, to Brussels and London. I even saw her in concert when I was heavily pregnant with each of my daughters. I've stayed up to the wee hours of the morning dancing to her songs in Antarctica on an icebreaker, to dancing to her songs on table tops in the Caribbean on Necker. I also turn to her music when I need comforting—it soothes my soul.

She is a legend who has stood the test of time, releasing one hit album after another, decade on decade. But people really don't give her credit for all that she has achieved. Her acting career had begun a few years before her singing one, and as a young teenager she would often cry backstage after being yelled at by producers. She is no flash in the pan; building a career with such longevity is about more than just pop music, it is also about being a smart businesswoman who is able to constantly reinvent herself. It requires resilience, endurance and getting up every single time she's been knocked down. And she has been knocked down plenty. She's had to reinvent herself, hearing the critics constantly and not letting them get to her.

There are lots of parallels to draw between Kylie's career and those of other high-performing people, be they stars, athletes, or entrepreneurs like myself. I look up to her because she's received so much criticism, particularly from her own countrymen, and yet she's prevailed. She was dubbed the "Singing Budgie" by the Australian media, and the nickname has followed her through the years. Yet, she has a professional approach, works hard to be the best at her game, and is real and authentic. She has confidence, or has found confidence in who she is and where she stands.

There are so many parts of Kylie's career and success that I resonate with and admire deeply. It is more than just her music. It is everything she embodies. Being herself and being real is her power, her secret weapon. I've learnt that it is mine too. Being yourself is so powerful; but it appears it isn't always that easy for people to do.

Have you heard the expression: "The tall poppy gets cut down?" If an Australian is perceived to be doing too well, especially overseas, other Australians begin ignoring news about or even resenting them. It's as if they've 'moved on' from Australia itself, as Kylie Minogue did—she became big in the UK, even a sort of honorary Brit in the eyes of the public, while her own countrymen pulled her down.

I'm a proud Australian and I love my home country, and this behaviour can be seen anywhere. But I think we are at risk if we don't look outside of our own countries to understand the bigger world which we live in. Yes, we should embrace our nation and what it stands for; but we should also look to the rest of the world and not have our blinkers on.

Unfortunately, when you do take those blinkers off you are at risk. Some of the treatment you get along the way will be difficult to bear. But that's how you expand yourself, through testing your resilience and mettle. For example, I've always had a fascination with Asia since I was a little girl, and I made my dream come true by living in Japan right after finishing high school. It was difficult and there were many times when I questioned what in the world I'd gotten myself into. It would have been easier if I'd just graduated and went on to university, hung out with my girlfriends and so on. My experience went against everything that was standard to what a young Australian girl should have done in those years. And I grew because of it.

This Girl, Kylie's song, is all about feeling confident in your own skin. It's about acknowledging who you are, and knowing that you should not give in.

Don't try to fit in with the rest. Instead, be proud to stand apart and be "this girl" who's authentic and real. That is immensely important to me, and has been the central theme running through my life.

People who are true to themselves are the ones who get through all the way to the finish line. Think about Sir Richard Branson, whose incredible authenticity and zest for life carries over into every one of his brands. This comfort in your own skin and ability to follow your own path without being swayed by others isn't easy, but it's how you stay honest to yourself and your underlying values. All my decision-making flows from my value system, not what someone else says or does.

No one is going to run your business for you, not even when you really wish someone else could sort the mess out for you! When things don't go as planned, when nothing works out, you need to dig deep. Do you really believe in what you are doing? Are you going to back yourself no matter what?

I believe in trusting my gut instincts, leading with the heart and being yourself. I think it's all interconnected with your purpose, what gets you out of bed in the morning, what drives you, and what motivates you in order to live a life that's true to yourself. Be this girl, not the one they want you to be.

SUCCESS TAKES GRIT

I'm proud that I had the courage to take my business beyond Australia, and made it thrive in an international market. I'm proud to be doing what I'm doing in Singapore and Asia, and to be recognised for it. It hasn't been an easy journey; it has been incredibly tough, and just the story of attracting global work here warrants an entire section to itself. I've thought so many times that I was going to fail, and I ruminated over what would happen if I did.

There are more challenges still to come. I write this while in the thick of the COVID-19 pandemic, and I've often considered leaving Singapore and returning to the rest of my family in Australia.

Even if that were to happen, I think the fact that I've achieved my goals and created a unique, sustainable business means that I've established something solid. God knows how many nights I've lain in bed, twisted in my sheets in a sweaty (sometimes teary) mess, with endless professional and personal lists running through my mind. Whether it is the day-to-day planning for the girls, or running through my client's latest campaign strategies, this is the ugly reality that most business owners don't talk about. It is not all champagne popping and confetti, my darlings!

I've not had a day off this entire year and sometimes, when I feel like I'm on the verge of a breakdown, my trusty meditation app helps me to relax and not implode. I've to remind myself that I'm not a machine that can keep running on empty. That's why true grit is needed when you're running your own business.

My business, Manning & Co., has received several awards over the last few years and I'm extremely humbled by this. I am also extremely grateful for Singapore Prime Minister Lee Hsien Loong's special reference to Gemstar at the 2018 Asean Summit in Sydney, about the work we are doing championing the Singapore and Australia relationship[1]. But what's also a great sign of success is being able to leverage those achievements and the businesses I've created to make positive change in the world.

I've developed a real-world Young Entrepreneurs Programme (YoungGems®) and had the pleasure of being the first to offer such a programme to the deaf and hard of hearing community. This programme is, again, authentic. It's real-world, non-academic and developed from real life entrepreneur experiences.

I wouldn't have been able to do these programmes if I hadn't taken my business internationally. I've had the privilege of listening to the stories about the impact our programmes have had on the lives of others. But looking back on all these achievements, I wouldn't be doing any of this if I had not started my business as a 28-year-old being forced out of

---

[1] For the full speech, see: "PM Lee Hsien Loong at the SME Conference at The ASEAN-Australia Business Summit," Prime Minister's Office, Government of Singapore, 16 March 2018, at https://www.pmo.gov.sg/Newsroom/pm-lee-hsien-loong-sme-conference-asean-australia-business-summit.

my corporate job after coming back from maternity leave. None of those would have happened without the adversities I've been through. I see more and more now that every part of my story has led (and will lead) to a bigger life purpose that is gradually unfolding in time.

My professional achievements and social impact work bring me great joy—but I'm most proud of my family. I'm proud of the fact that I've such a deep connection and relationship with my girls, Mum and sister. I've got all my business achievements, but it's the personal milestones I've achieved along the way that make it complete.

I've managed to forge an enduring professional career and build my own thriving business and all that comes with that, all while raising these two beautiful girls despite setbacks at times in my life. It is truly gratifying to be complimented on how wonderful my girls are whenever anyone meets them. To maintain such a close and loving relationship with my mother who lives miles away in Australia, despite the busyness of our lives, is another achievement for me.

You've heard about positive thinking, and of the idea of putting your dreams and aspirations out to the universe. But it goes a step further than just creative visualisation, from my experience. When I don't have a clear goal, or when I don't act on the steps necessary to put these things in place, no matter how much I visualise the end-goal in my mind's eye, things just don't happen. But when I set the foundations and plan the specifics of the goal, even if it takes me some time to achieve it, I do reach it in the end.

Setting the goal is one thing. The drive and the fire in the belly needs to be there to see your plans to fruition too. Roadblocks will come and you have to overcome them somehow; I've experienced and seen how much effort and endurance it can take, and I haven't sanitised any of it. I've been through countless dark nights of the soul, and whatever your age or gender, I hope you'll find inspiration from my story.

There are so many good men in my life who have been amazing mentors on my journey. Men can be champions of change too in our collective efforts to achieve gender equality, and when I was conducting the Young Entrepreneurs Programme in Perth, Western Australia, I had equal numbers of both sexes participating. Quite a few of the young men were fascinated by my story, and wanted to find out even more about my experiences and journey through entrepreneurship.

They told me that even within the university environment, they'd experienced the macho pressure from the already existing 'boys' club' atmosphere. That power structure still exists in the world of business *and* the tertiary school setting that feeds it, and its influence on what it takes to be a man with it. This is concerning, given that we need to change perceptions in the young generations for real change to occur.

It also dawned on me that not all young men subscribe to those antiquated ideas. And more than that, they actually *want* to be different from those stereotypes set out by male peer pressure. They want to map out their own authentic course, and don't want to adhere to the standard norms of how you treat men and women in certain environments.

There is no doubt that that these institutional structures continue to dominate, but young people have the power to change that. And it is my hope that stories like mine will help spread the word that there can be another way beyond what is currently accepted to be bog standard. May you find some gems of knowledge and inspiration in the following pages.

Enjoy!

With love,

Gemma

PART ONE

LAYING THE FOUNDATION

CHAPTER ONE
AN UNUSUAL START

You will be defined not just by what you achieve,

but by how you survive.

— Sheryl Sandberg

Eleven and 22 are both master numbers in the numerology belief system, and I've both in my birthday. They are quite significant for those who believe in numerology.

I was born on 22 November 1979 in Sydney, Australia, with my zodiac sign right on the cusp of Scorpio and Sagittarius. That apparently signified that I embody qualities of both signs: bold, passionate, and capable. According to numerology, after adding up all the numbers of my birthdate, I've life path number 5:

> Life Path Number 5 is the number of freedom and change, and those with a Life Path of 5 tend to seek freedom above all else. They are adventurers, having a restless nature, and being on the go, constantly seeking change and variety in life. They have a free spirit and need to have variety in their day.[2]

I've a bit of a spiritual bent, and both my zodiac and numerology details always attract great excitement from those who follow these systems closely. But despite the auspicious astrology surrounding my birth, I had a traumatic start to life—my mother almost lost me before I was born.

When Mum was five months pregnant with me, she lost her own mother quite suddenly. Mum was an only child and she was very close to her mother *and* grandmother—two instrumental role models and figures in her life. She woke up early one morning to a phone call from her stepfather: "Darling, you might want to come over here quickly. I've

---

[2] "Life Path Number 5," *Seventh Life Path*, at https://seventhlifepath.com/numerology/life-path-number-5.

some news about Mummy." My grandmother had suffered a heart attack after having choked, and subsequently died. She was only 52.

Mum was 27, and she had lost the most important person in her life. With my own Mum being the most important person in my life, I simply can't fathom such a loss.

My mum had an unconventional upbringing for 1950s Australia. She was an only child, in a baby boom that meant most families had more than one child. To add to this, her parents had divorced when she was very young. She never got the chance to get to know her biological father until he came back into her life when she was 16. Unfortunately, he was dying of bone cancer at the time, leaving little time to get to know him.

This was the year that Mum and my dad met. Having already lost her father at such a young age, losing her remaining parent just slightly over a decade later was a devastating blow. 3 July remains a very hard day for my mother, even 40 years on.

Her grief from losing her mother was so overwhelming that she was hospitalised with bronchitis. The trauma over losing her sole remaining parent was too much and doctors warned that she could easily lose her unborn baby—me.

Despite her grief of losing the most important person in her life, Mum had to find the resilience and strength to keep going. Despite her pregnancy, she had to keep working at her late mother's news agency business until she could sell it. Every morning at 4 am, she pulled herself out of bed and drove across Sydney to make sure that all the newspaper delivery orders were ready for sale. She worked through those few months of absolute hell right up to my birth on 22 November.

Those precious few months before your baby's birth are meant to be a special time, something that I know all too well from my experiences with my own two girls. But this was an incredibly bittersweet time for Mum. It was a heart-breaking time in her life that took its toll on her.

I came into the world during that incredibly stressful and traumatic period, but my birth is what helped Mum get through. Mum still says it was the most joyous occasion, and I bought such light and happiness. She says that I was an absolute gift because it was almost as if I knew what she was going through. I was the happiest and most easy-going baby, feeding and sleeping well. It was as if I was in tune with what had been happening on the outside. My very being was considered an extension of the most important person in my mum's world. To this day I still call my late maternal grandmother my 'Big Nanny'. I've kept her spirit alive.

I still feel very sad that I didn't get the chance to meet my grandmother and grow up with her in my life. I know that we would have got along like two peas in a pod! Big Nanny had always been a woman well ahead of her time. She simply did not belong to her era—she wasn't going to settle as a housewife in the 1950s, as she was far too modern and forward-thinking. I'm told that I'm a lot like her; I look like her, share her unruly curly thick hair, and her wild determination and drive.

Big Nanny was a leader—she had her own path and did things her way. She wasn't going to fit the mould for the sake of fitting in. Things like divorcing (when divorce was still frowned upon) and running her own businesses in male-dominated sectors when business leadership wasn't something women did. She had a string of businesses in fact: a laundromat, a manufacturer of school desks and a news agency. She was a truly remarkable woman whom I would have loved to have met.

GROWING UP YEARS

My mum tells me the story of how I used to love to be close and cuddle as a baby. I still do! When I was just shy of turning one, I had worked out how to climb out of my cot with the view that I was going to find my way to my parents' room for a cuddle. Mum eventually found out what I was doing, as one morning she came into my room only to find me sleeping against the door. I used to push my blanket through the gaps in the cot and climb down the other side to shimmy my way out. I was doggedly determined to find my way to my mama.

Once Mum had cottoned on to what I was doing, she used to leave pillows and cushions on the ground knowing that night after night I would throw myself out of the cot to get to her. I was in a grown bed a few months later. I'm still a very tactile person—my girls call me the "most kissiest Mummy" in the world. I love cuddles and closeness, and that determination has never left me.

I've some very vivid memories of my early years and remember Mum's own grandmother— another strong female influence early on. I know her as my Little Nanny, and she played the role of a grandmother and looked after me at times. I remember her famous cheese and pickle sandwiches that I simply loved! She unfortunately died when I was three, another loss for Mum. Although I was only three, I remember being incredibly upset at the news of her passing.

I also have early memories of my mum working. I know I get my strong work ethic from her and the women who came before me in my family. None of them were afraid of hard work, and all strived for financial independence. When I was little, Mum started a cleaning business. Mum would take a portable cot and some toys with her and in I would go—I never made a fuss. I would keep myself busy until Mum was finished with her work, and she did such a good job during that time and built a loyal clientele.

When I was five, Mum and Dad separated. Every divorce has its own story, which I've come to understand from my own personal experience. Mum and Dad got together when they were so young, as did Tristan (my girls' dad) and me. Sometimes people simply grow apart and are not meant to be for the long haul, like us.

Years later, I look back and realise that my own life has mirrored elements of my mother's life. My mum raised two girls singlehandedly and was even around the same age that I was when Tristan and I separated, when she separated from Dad. It was a rather bizarre turn of events, and I'm just thankful that the similarities did not extend to me losing her. I can't imagine losing my mother or welcoming one of my girls into the world without her around.

I love my mum, no doubt the way she loved hers. And my girls have the closest relationship with her—it is beautiful, full of love, mischief and closeness, something I did not have growing up with a grandparent.

After Mum and Dad divorced, we saw Dad every other weekend. I have very fond memories from the time spent with him. We would go to Sydney's Powerhouse Museum (a historic museum featuring exhibits of both sciences and the arts) and participate in a lot of outdoor activities together. Dad was hopeless at cooking, so I also remember weekends with him eating Space Sticks, and special trips to McDonald's on George Street, or milkshakes at Broadway's Grace Brothers!

My mum remarried a few years later, this time to a self-made man—a real entrepreneur of the time. DR had left school at 12 and had worked hard for everything that he had built. Despite the serious flaws that would become apparent later, I admire him for that. He ran several butcheries and farms raising cattle, sheep and pigs. Mum supported his entrepreneurial pursuits so when he wanted to start a fish farm, we moved to Cairns in far north Queensland. I was eight and my sister Natalie was 12.

Our life in Cairns was very different from those early years in Sydney. It opened our eyes to a different life. In Cairns, we experienced living close to some of the great wonders of Australia—the Great Barrier Reef was at our doorstep, as was the Daintree Rainforest. We spent weekends with friends sailing, visiting the close-by islands like Green Island, snorkelling at Agincourt Reef, and spending time at Port Douglas.

It was a lovely time in my childhood. Our fish farm was stunning and was located on the most beautiful property at the bottom of the Great Dividing Range. It was spread across five hectares and was full of tropical vegetation and life! We grew mangos, macadamia nuts, bananas, five corner fruit, blackberries and the list goes on. We also had the most exotic pets as animals—from Liberarchi and Lola, the peacocks, to Diana and

Charles, the geese. Then there were the guinea fowls too. It was a very different upbringing.

I loved farm life. I especially would love coming home from school with my sister and helping Mum around the farm. I would quickly get changed out of my school uniform into my home clothes and would either feed the fish in the dams, or catch any tadpoles that may have started breeding in our ponds. I knew everything about breeding tropical fish by the age of 10, learning from Mum who had become an expert in water chemistry, and in the delicate techniques and intricacies of breeding tropical fish!

I absolutely adored my time in Cairns, for the friends I made and the unique experiences I had. It was a growing time. I feel very fortunate for having had such an enriching and eventful childhood. It wasn't boring to say the very least!

Strangely enough, looking back, my eventual move to Singapore was like my family's move to Cairns. Both places feel similar to me. With Cairns being located at the northern part of Australia, the climate is very humid and tropical, much like in Singapore. When I look out at the lipstick palms from my living room now in Singapore, it transports me back to those years in Cairns. It's strange how the chips fell.

We lived in Cairns for about four years, and it became a significant period in my life, influencing a great deal of what shaped me. This was the 1980s, and Cairns was a very popular destination for the Japanese. There was a real boom, with them buying up a lot of real estate, golf courses and hotels. Businesses were flush with Japanese money. Learning a European language at school in Cairns in the 1980s wasn't a thing like it was in Sydney, and in Cairns, Japanese was the language to learn. Both Natalie and I loved learning Japanese. Japan would eventually become an important part of my later life—for all sorts of reasons.

Life in Cairns was a nice break from the rat-race living of Sydney. Cairns is far more relaxed than the big city life of Sydney. The weather is warm all year round. Natalie and I rode our bikes everywhere and it was safe, like Singapore; in those years, Sydney saw many crimes, like break-ins, assaults and other creepy incidents.

Moving to Cairns was a breath of fresh air in more ways than one. We formed beautiful friendships that we still have to this day. Trinity Anglican School (TAS) was where my sister and I went to study. Cairns, like Singapore, is a very transient city. You had people from all over the world, but also people from other parts of Australia, coming to work and stay for a period. It felt truly international, with the myriad of cultures we were encountering at school and in the neighbourhood. During those years, my dad would come up to visit us, and occasionally we would go back to Sydney for holidays.

It was not all positive, of course. I was bullied at the first school I went to, being picked on because I was "too smart". This happened because I was placed in a composite class consisting of students from year 1-3, and there were only a few 8-year-olds like me in that class. There was no focus on teaching us older kids, and I had by then already read all the books that they gave us.

I struggled with the initial adjustment and had to learn resilience and adaptability; all while being relentlessly bullied. In the end, I struck up a friendship with a younger Islander girl, and her older brother protected me from the bullies. I moved schools after six months and went to another local school, before I finally got into TAS where Natalie was already studying at. Things were a lot better there, and by then I had the necessary skills to tide me through the "new girl" blues. Natalie and I were happy in Cairns, with our school and our friends. We really did not want to return to Sydney.

But we did eventually, to open a retail aquarium. Cairns was where we bred goldfish and tropical fish, which we then supplied to many retail aquariums across Australia. We were moving back because we were going to have our own retail outlet.

Now here is another interesting hint to my eventual path in life. My mum made her first trip to Singapore when I was about eight or so, to study the fish farms. One of their business partners back then was a Singaporean man, who helped them with the ins-and-outs of the business. It became quite successful and Mum left her job in the pharmacy to help run the fish farm business. (She had sold Big Nanny's news agency when I was born, and then later started a career working in pharmacy.)

While it was expected for women not to work when they had children, my mum always did. She was so used to being independent and having her own money that she would not stop working. She started a cleaning business when I was a baby so that she could always have me with her while she worked.

By the time we moved to Cairns, Mum had been working for some time at the pharmacy just up the road from where we lived, a place she could work and still be close to us. When we moved to Cairns, she had to leave that job and sell our house in Sydney.

This is partly the reason why I'm so passionate about businesses and projects to do with independent female entrepreneurs. My mum had sold everything and put it all into the fish farm in Cairns. She took full responsibility for raising my sister and me. She paid for our school fees, fed and clothed us, and she put every bit of sweat into the fish farm because she supported DR's dream.

We had sold everything in Sydney and invested it all into Cairns. And then we left it all again to come back to Sydney. On returning to Sydney, I finished Year Six in the school that I left, before I started high school. Nat went into Year Ten at Riverside Girls' School, but didn't really know too many people as we had been away for years. The transition back was hard, and took adjusting to. We missed our beloved Cairns. I would cry myself to sleep most nights and have photos of my friends close to me, so I wouldn't forget them or the special time that I had living there.

LOSING IT ALL

Although the purpose for moving back to Sydney was to open a retail aquarium, unfortunately not everything went to plan. During this time,

DR showed another side to him. Some people take a bit of time to reveal their true selves, and by the time DR did, Mum had already invested so much into his dreams that the fall-out was devastating.

The turning point came when I was in Melbourne to see my dad. By that point, Dad had remarried, and had another daughter. Later Dad moved from Sydney to Melbourne for his work, and he still lives in Melbourne today. My daughters actually refer to him as 'Melbie'—a name that has come to stick with Nat's children too.

One school holiday when I was about 14, I travelled with my school friend to stay with Dad in Melbourne. Whilst I was away, my older sister was at home with Mum. Nat was studying for her final high school year exams when she witnessed something we could never forgive. DR had gotten into a rage about something and thrown Mum against the wall, and her body slammed painfully against the cement. The incident gave her problems with her upper back and shoulders that persist to this day. My sister saw everything. It was an incredibly traumatic time and it was the straw that broke the camel's back.

That was the end of the marriage. Mum had supported DR and his dreams and changed her world for him. But she would not put up with his antics and aggressive behaviour any longer.

It was not a pleasant time. The divorce was messy—DR had engaged the best solicitors from the top law firm in Sydney to represent him. Mum could not afford such good representation and in the end, she lost almost everything as he came out on top, winning most of their shared assets. Despite my mum selling her Sydney home and funding the start of the fish business, she wasn't fairly compensated. They came to some settlement over our beautiful fish farm in Cairns, and then she was forced to buy the aquarium business from him. Right after settling the property in Cairns, she had to use her part of the money to pay him for the business.

My mum lost so much at this point—everything that she had worked so hard for was taken from her. My mum worked from a very young age and had saved every cent in order to buy her first home with Dad, a house that was formerly my grandmother's. Mum had worked so hard to buy this first property, then our family home in Abbotsford, and then had put all she had left into our lives in Cairns... only to lose practically everything. As a family, we have never forgiven what DR did to us.

Mum had already been through hell and back. We moved from our waterfront apartment to above the aquarium—a warehouse style building located in an unattractive part of Sydney. It was on a major highway and was selected because of the high traffic flow, not with living there in mind. Smart for a business decision, but not the best for a residential one. Overnight, things had changed so much.

All of this happened around Christmas and though Mum always loved spoiling us, she did not have the money that year. I think we each received a pair of pyjamas.

Despite all of that, she made the best of everything. She is a woman who has got absolute grace, with impeccable taste and style. And she made our apartment above the shop look like a million-dollar loft in New York, without spending very much. Mum has taught me you don't always need money to dress well or for things to look good. Style is something from within.

In those early days of adjusting to this next phase, it came to light quite quickly that Mum had just paid for a business that was deep in debt. DR had kept two sets of books for the business, and while she had paid a substantial amount for it, she did not realise that had come with such crippling debt. And so, the creditors came knocking and the business was very close to liquidation. Some of her suppliers came by with papers to say, "Surely you know of this situation. This is everything that you owe us." Mum was absolutely horrified; she had neither knowledge nor a hint of awareness of how much trouble the business was in.

One of her biggest suppliers even sent somebody to take over the business. We had just lost our home and were new to this place. Finding out that the business was in such a bad shape was extremely stressful. Even when my parents were separating, I don't remember it in such trouble. I was younger then. I was older now and this was totally different.

But it was during this period that we experienced such extremes. We had experienced the great highs and terrible lows; going from sailing on a beautiful yacht and living on an idyllic tropical farm and the Sydney waterfront to this. That was when I first truly began to understand that things can happen in life that you don't set out or plan for—it's how you respond to such unexpected events that is key.

My mum has had to hold herself together throughout her life; she oozes style and grace, but also has a lot of grit. She carried on magnificently through it all. But I've seen her break down—understandably so. DR was aggressive and heartless, and to leave us in this situation was a clear power play on his part.

Mum must have been in her early forties at that point, and I saw as a young teenager how relationships could play out. I value independence (especially financial independence) even more now after seeing what my mother has gone through, and how she worked so hard to get everything in her life only to have it all snatched away from her. It was so unfair.

It has been lovely to see Mum discover her passion and calling later in life in the interior business. She now works in the textiles sector of the interior design industry, and is highly regarded and well respected. She has found her calling and excels at what she does.

I value how my mum has carried herself through everything. She is vivacious, fun, warm and loving. She lights up a room with her smile, and always has everyone captivated.

I'm *purpose*-driven not money-driven, although financial independence is definitely important to me and something I believe is important for everyone, especially women. When I was growing up, I always had goals around saving money.

MAKING MONEY MOVES

I had my first job when I was 12 years old, when we were still living in our waterfront Sydney apartment. I would babysit for a neighbour who worked nights, and needed someone to watch her 8-year-old daughter. The girl was neglected and desperate for some nurturing, and even though I was only 12, I took this little girl under my wing and looked after her.

During those evenings, I would eat my dinner with her and then go back upstairs to do my homework, before going down to their apartment to start babysitting around 8.30 pm. Sometimes, I would sleep there for the night when her mother had a particularly long working night, and when the woman came home in the morning, I would return upstairs to get ready for school.

Babysitting made me my first A$1,000, and I liked looking after and caring for the little girl. Her mother treated us well, and once my sister and I were given tickets to a Madonna concert and asked to take her daughter. We were driven there in a red Ferrari—who would forget that!

From a young age, I wanted to save money and pay for things myself. I was very mindful of the importance of finance and personal savings. I'd always worried about making sure that we had enough to look after ourselves. We had a comfortable living, but up to a point. Mum was effectively a single mother. She was also fiercely independent, and raised us with little help from anyone. Once we were grocery shopping in Cairns, and I remember putting things back on the shelves and telling her, "Mum, we don't need this or that."

I was very conscious and mindful of spending, always making sure that we were within our means even when we had it good in those years. Extravagance has never been my style, and I've never lived beyond my means.

You had to be at least 14 years and nine months old to legally work part-time in Australia and when I hit that age, I started to work in a café every Sunday. After that, my first retail job was with Spotlight, a famous Australian chain selling hobby craft materials. Even during my final school years, I worked my part-time job and saved everything I earned. As a prefect in Year Twelve, I gave a speech to the next senior year of students about the importance of having a balanced approach to the final year in school, including part-time work.

Many of my friends in those years were not working as they were only focused on studying. But though I had those part-time jobs, I still made time to be a regular teenager, doing my schoolwork and hanging out with my girlfriends on the weekends.

I was a very conscientious and dedicated student while in school. My love for the Japanese language continued despite my school in Sydney not offering it, so I had lessons on Saturdays at another school, and later by correspondence. (This was before the Internet was advanced enough to support language lessons.) I was determined to keep up my language skills because I loved it—I'm no longer as fluent as I used to be, but my love for Japan remains.

Despite the fact that I loved writing, my Year Twelve English teacher made her lessons thoroughly unpleasant. I had told her that I wanted to be a journalist, and her answer was: "You're not good enough in English. You wouldn't make it." What a horrid thing to say to a student!

I did not let that stop me. My determination, serious goal setting, and absolute relentless ambition and dedication to achieving my aspirations won out. If somebody tells me I can't do something, I will dig deeper and prove them wrong. And that was exactly what I did to that teacher, scoring excellent marks in English in our final-year high school exams, and doing well enough to get into the communications course I wanted.

My school years had a bittersweet ending. By the time our examination results came out, I had already moved to Japan—I wasn't even there in Sydney with my friends to receive them, or celebrate having done so well.

Mum had to go to school on my behalf to get the award, so I never had the satisfaction of going back to see the look on my old English teacher's face. But it didn't really matter, because in a way I had already moved on. I was deep in another adventure, in a country I had come to love so much.

CHAPTER TWO
BEING BOLD

> I always did something I was a little not ready to
> do. I think that's how you grow. When there's that
> moment of "Wow, I'm not really sure I can do this,"
> and you push through those moments, that's when
> you have a breakthrough.
>
> — Marissa Mayer

In the 1990s, many Australians went to Japan to teach English, especially following the boom of Japan's economy in the 1980s. There was a programme called Japan Exchange and Teaching (JET), where applicants from other countries could travel to Japan to teach English. But I wanted to do something out of the mainstream, so I chose a more unstructured programme where you could go to Japan on a working holiday, teaching English at ski resorts to the locals.

I was 18, due to leave for Japan just two weeks after my end of school and before Christmas in 1997. In my case, I was assigned at the last moment to work not at a ski resort, but at a resort on the island of Hatsushima.

I only found out the details when I arrived in Japan. I had just finished my school exams, turned 18 and had two weeks to celebrate my end of school before I was due to fly to Japan and leave my life as I knew it. Mum tried to convince me to stay in Australia until the next intake for the programme in April. But I knew that if I had left it for a few months, I probably wouldn't have gone. I would have to do it right then, or else end up getting too comfortable.

The time leading up to my departure was painful. I had met Tristan (who would eventually become the father of my girls) at the beginning of that year, and we were already in a relationship by then. "I'm going to Japan, and I'm just letting you know that nothing is going to stop me," I told him upfront. "Nothing is going to get in my way!"

When the day came, while all my friends were enjoying their school break and going away to spend time with each other as newly liberated adolescents, I was on my way to this grand adventure abroad. I had a teddy bear which Mum gave me, wearing a beautiful message on its scarf. The message said, "Darling Gemma, congratulations on this big journey and adventure! I am so proud of you. When you need me, Teddy will be there for you giving you big hugs and lots of love. Love you so much, Mama xx."

This teddy bear came on the plane with me and I hugged it so tightly on my lap as the plane took off. The reality of it all finally hit me then. "Wow, I'm really doing this. What have I done?" I wondered. I had said many emotional goodbyes, and that high quickly faded and gave way to a sickness in my stomach.

I remember vividly arriving at Narita Airport, and the journey to a YMCA in Tokyo with my cohort. That night all the others went out to experience the nightlife in Tokyo, but all I wanted to do was finish my copy of *Memoirs of a Geisha*. In the end, I couldn't pick up the book—it had been a present and reminded me too much of home and what I had left behind.

I tried going for a traditional sauna called an *onsen*, and there I got my first culture shock. Not only would I be bathing in the nude with a group of strange women, I would have to face them with eyes bloodshot from all the tears. I took myself back to my bunk and cried myself to sleep. I felt empty, sick and alone. Despite having studied the Japanese language and culture for a decade, I realised now how foreign it still was.

I had travelled to Bali two years before with my schoolmates, but Japan was a whole different ballgame. I was sent off to work at Hatsushima, which was a ferry ride from the town of Atami—itself more than an hour's drive from Tokyo.

Hatsushima is a tiny island, only about four kilometres across—and I arrived there as the only foreigner. It was hardcore and I only had a day to settle in. I lived and worked on the island, sleeping and eating in a little dormitory after working long hours. My role was in guest services as the token *gaijin*, or foreigner. Part of my job was greeting holidaymakers or conference guests coming to the island; I would bow to them as they exited their buses. I wore a tropical-inspired uniform as if I should have been working in Hawaii, despite the freezing temperature. It was winter when I first arrived, and I would have to go outside in the freezing cold and greet every passenger, bowing and directing them inside the hotel.

There was a golf course, a marina and aquatic sports, but otherwise there was little we could do on our downtime. We could head to the island's small village or the little pub nearby, but that was it.

What had led me there in the first place? When I started learning Japanese as an 8-year-old, I had promised myself that I would learn the language one day in Japan. I still don't know if that stubborn goal-setting was a strength or weakness, but I can explain it at least. It's when I set myself these goals that I often push myself out of my comfort zone and grow as a result—you might call it a growth mindset. That fear of the unknown and yearning for familiar comforts reminded me how far out of it I had gone, but it was what I knew I had to do.

That didn't stop me from losing 5 kg from homesickness. Some days I just felt my resolve wavering; other times I constantly wondered what was happening at home with Tristan, my family and my friends, comparing their full lives to my isolation and lack of anyone to speak English with.

At times I was very frightened. One time, I was woken up at 3 am with everything in my small, tiny apartment crashing down. There had been a bad earthquake close by and we could feel the tremors on the island. It was the first time I had experienced something like that. For a moment, I thought that was the end. Things finally settled, and I fell back asleep. We often experienced tremors on the island and one time I felt the earth literally move underneath me.

I did get some comfort from the few friends I made on the island. Back then, communication was not as instantaneous as it is today—all we had was a fax machine and a telephone. International calling fees were expensive to utilise often, so I used to anticipate every single fax that Mum or Tristan sent.

The day my high school examination results were announced, Mum called me in a state of excitement.

"Darling, I've got your results from school!" she told me.

There I was, in this tiny dormitory, shaking. Was it from fear that I would not do well? Nervousness? I was so alone.

"Okay, Mum. How'd I do?"

"Darling, you got 95.3!" It was better than I had expected! In a way, I owed it to my teachers who gave me that push to do so well, simply by telling me I wasn't good enough.

There was nobody in the little dormitory to share the good news with, let alone share in its gravitas. I celebrated my first huge milestone achievement on my own. And it brought me back to reality—one can have an amazing achievement, but life must go on.

A CHANGE IN SCENERY

"This is just too hard," I thought to myself often. The isolation, constant use of Japanese and full-on busyness of the job took its toll, but what really made me want out were the unsavoury and scary bits of my work compounding with them.

Many Japanese businessmen came to Hatsushima for R&R visits, and as a foreigner, I was seen as an exotic specimen. Some of them even grabbed me and tried to pull me into their rooms! I had to pry their fingers off me, wrestle them away and run off. There was no one to protect vulnerable young women from them.

"Yuriko, I can't do this for another six months," I confided to my friend. I was meant to be at the island for a year, but by the halfway point I could not go on.

"Gemma, I don't think you should go home just yet. You are doing so well with your Japanese," she said. "You came all this way, so let me try to find another job for you." And bless her, she did. Looking back, even though the pull to go home was so great, I'm so glad that I stayed longer and fought through. What happened next was life-changing in many ways.

Yuriko would be my way of getting off the island. My boss was a good, understanding man named Mr Fujiwara, but despite his concern for me, his hands were tied by a difficult contract to get out of, and the powers above him. I had to be strong and stand my ground, and even more so to get my last pay check from the organisation. (Mr Fujiwara remained a good friend, and would visit me in Australia years later.)

There were a few good people there for sure, and I did make some good friends. But most people who went there tended to treat it as a stepping stone to get to a better, different type of work.

One of Yuriko's friends operated an establishment in Karuizawa, located north of Tokyo. Karuizawa is almost like a spiritual home for her because she used to do her summer part-time jobs there. It's a beautiful, magical place where the wealthy people from Tokyo have their holiday homes because it is so high up in the mountains. The temperature is comfortably cool there during the summer, when the weather gets very humid in Tokyo. It is a beautiful place to spend the summer.

That was my ticket in. "I'm going to see if I can get you a job there. They'll be really busy in the summer, and my friend might be able to put you up to stay and let you work in his restaurant."

It worked out. By the time I was ready to leave, Tristan was visiting and accompanied me to the train station in Shinjuku. I knew I had to keep going, even if I really just wanted to go home. I caught the bullet train with my faithful teddy bear, and arrived at Karuizawa.

I really did not know what to expect. When I got out of the train and walked through the station, I saw an older lady who looked as if she was searching for somebody. She spotted me and asked in Japanese: "Gemma-chan? Are you Gemma?"

I hadn't been expecting a woman to be looking after me—Yuriko's friend Aichan was a man. It turned out her name was Koitabashi-san, and she was a close friend Aichan had asked to look after me.

Aichan and Koitabashi became a surrogate family to me. Koitabashi was the caretaker of Mitsubishi's then holiday retreat in Karuizawa, housed in a sprawling property at the base of a volcano with a beautiful lake. Besides a residence, it also boasted an art gallery and a library, and traditional Japanese homes with tatami mats and *onsens*. During the summer, Mitsubishi used to send all their employees there on a holiday retreat.

She was the caretaker of the whole place. She cooked, cleaned—she did everything. (During that summer of 1998, because Japan was going through a bad time with the economy, Mitsubishi had to stop using this property as their official holiday retreat.)

"Gemma-chan, I'm going to look after you," she told me. "You don't need to pay me for accommodation or anything. In return, I've lots of friends with lots of different businesses whom you can go and help occasionally."

And so, I did. I ended up living with Koitabashi for the rest of my time in Japan in this most amazing, incredible, historic place. It was just her and me living within the grounds of this beautiful property, and I became like her daughter. She became my *okaasan*, my 'other mother'.

LIFE WITH MY ADOPTED *OKAASAN*

The stability that my Japanese mum provided allowed me to consistently venture out of my comfort zone and open up to all the new experiences Japan had to offer. She watched me take it all in, and encouraged it.

At one point, she called in a favour with the Mayor of the area we lived in, so I could participate in a local Matsuri—an occasion for offering thanks and praise to a deity at a shrine. It comes from a word meaning 'to entertain' or 'to serve'. As part of a Matsuri, there is a *mikoshi* (a portable altar or shrine that is walked around the town). It effectively is taking the deity out to see the people.

Traditionally, only boys and men are involved in the procession. But on this occasion my Japanese mum had received permission for me to participate—the first time ever for a woman, and only because I was a visitor and a guest of the Mayor's friend.

I wore a special kimono with a matching headband wrapped around my head, and off I was carried. I stood at the front of the *mikoshi*, as some

20 or 30 carried the shrine on their shoulders. They would sometimes toss it (and me) into the air, and I held on for dear life!

My *okaasan* was determined to ensure I could experience all that I could. As another strong female force and influence in my life, she was always willing to push boundaries as a female herself. Nothing was going to get in the way of her Gemma-chan experiencing all that she could while in Japan.

When I wasn't being tossed in the air at special festivals, I had every part-time job you could imagine. I worked in a *sushi* place, a *ramen* shop and even a mini-hotel called a pensione. Besides that, I helped Koitabashi with her duties in the library and the gallery.

I also went to help Aichan in his restaurant, known as Kinoko—the Japanese word for 'mushroom', from the two mushroom-shaped little huts on a piece of property that Koitabashi owned. He effectively became my Japanese dad.

He was my protector, Koitabashi my carer. Kinoko was quite an exclusive restaurant, and it was so good that people would have to find him and persuade him to open it if they wanted to eat there. He only opened when he felt like it, which made for some very irregular hours. The Beatle John Lennon and his wife Yoko Ono had been frequent customers, when they went to Japan to escape from the paparazzi. Aichan kept their memorabilia on display in his restaurant, including a cup Lennon had drunk from.

He was an incredibly eccentric man and I did not realise that Aichan and Koitabashi were in a relationship at first. All I knew was that my Japanese mum lived on an amazing property, and was incredibly clever as she had saved her money and bought the property where Kinoko had been built. Aichan used to come by to the Mitsubishi property just to use the *onsens*, bringing his own little toiletry kit. I used to think it was very odd that he would come and just help himself to the baths, as I merely thought that they were very close friends.

Living in Karuizawa, I had the unique experience of getting very close to these people. I would ride my bike to Aichan's restaurant and help him there with different jobs, and in the process established the strongest of bonds. My mum was so grateful that I had this lovely lady come into my life to look after me that she sent a beautiful cross-stitch of our home in Cairns as a gift to her. It sat framed up in Kinoko, taking pride of place there. I often wonder if it is still there.

Unfortunately, I've lost contact with my Japanese family and don't know what has happened to them. I used to go back to Japan regularly because I really missed it, and that was when I finally pieced together the story of my adopted Japanese family. They really were together, but they could never be public about their relationship because he was 10 years younger than her. In a way, I suppose she was his sugar mama as she was incredibly good with her money, managing this Mitsubishi house retreat. When I met her, she must have been in her fifties. She had saved up all her money when she was younger, and had bought that property that Kinoko was built on. It was actually her property and not his.

She had built the two huts so that one day, when she retired from running things for Mitsubishi, she would stay in one hut and the other would house Aichan and his restaurant. There was an understanding—an underlying rule or agreement that they would grow old together and have this for themselves. Nobody wanted to acknowledge this relationship even if deep down they knew about it, as it was still very taboo in Japan.

Aichan and Koitabashi would visit Australia twice after my return, and even came to my wedding, where I delivered a thank you speech to them in Japanese. It was truly special to have them in my life, and this love between Koitabashi and myself was deep and genuine. Koitabashi had no interest in children of her own, but she still bonded with me, the first foreigner she had ever met, as a surrogate daughter.

I know she was blown away by the deep connection and special bond we naturally formed—her brothers had served in World War 2, and it was a big deal for a *gaijin* to come into their world as much as I had. Nevertheless, they fully accepted me into their home and extended family. My Japanese was fluent enough by that time to have enriching conversations with everyone. I ended my sojourn in Japan knowing that it all meant something truly special. Yes, it was difficult, and sometimes terrifying going out of my comfort zone. I had been through so much, but what I gained from persevering to the end was absolutely beautiful.

I would love to go on a mission to find my adopted family again, wherever they are now. I don't even know if they're still around, but that will be another adventure to undertake soon.

HOMECOMING

That year in Japan changed me so much that upon returning to Australia, it all felt so different. I wasn't prepared for how I would feel. I was obviously looking forward to going home and seeing Mum, Nat and Tristan again, but on the whole, I felt so far removed from most of my friends, who had just done their first year of university.

I came back and struggled to fit in. I had grown so much during my time in Japan that I felt that although I was due to go to university myself, I just wanted to get it over with, then get into life and keep extending myself.

This was my first taste of feeling hugely different in a place that should be so familiar. Who does that to themselves? I had thrown myself into a challenging situation, ripping myself away from safety and entering a hard sometimes painful experience. It was natural to feel so out of sorts, in retrospect.

On my second day back in Australia, I got a job at the local Japanese restaurant. I'm not one to let the grass grow under my feet! Even though I had just returned from a life-changing experience, I did not give myself the time to analyse it all or figure out how best to fit in. I needed to get a job and get back into the groove of things. And I was firm that Japan needed to feature prominently in them.

Tristan and I stood the test of time and distance. We stuck together during that whole period, and he was my rock when I came back. Out of everybody amongst my peers, he was my constant and despite our time apart, he still felt familiar. Of course, he had grown and changed during that year, but he was the only one I felt like I could still belong with.

Although I'm book-smart and can reap excellent marks if I put my mind to it, I'm not academically inclined. I love working and like earning money, so that I can be financially independent and have the means to take care of myself and my family. I had the option of doing a five-year degree in International Studies, and through it I could have gone back to Japan to do a double degree. But I chose not to do that—five years was too long a time to spend studying for me.

The degree I chose at that time was called New Media Communications, and it was the first course in Australia that focused on new media such as Web development. I had assumed I was going to do a traditional PR Communications course, but most of the emphasis was on new media. And it is interesting to look back and see that it was the industry which I ended up doing business in.

My degree also included advanced Japanese. I did not ever get into the university scene; things like partying and going to student bars were not on my radar. I would only do university things in university; instead of partying, I worked part-time. I had different jobs outside of school, and I was still going out with Tristan through it all. I was there with a mission, and it was just another step to reach my goals.

When I turned 21, Tristan and I bought an apartment together. I had saved enough to pay the deposit on a little one-bedder, at an age when many of my friends were still living with their parents. Even better—Tristan was (and still is) a tradesman, and he had done a cabinet-making course while I was in Japan. At his workplace, they make kitchens, tables, and office furniture. With this skillset, we were able to renovate the whole apartment on our own, and made it delightful.

We lived there for two years, and then I had a bee in my bonnet to buy a house. A house across the road had come on the market. It was a deceased estate and was well-priced. "Let's buy it!" I told Tristan, and so we took the plunge. We sold the apartment and before we knew it, we had bought our first house in Sydney's up-and-coming inner city suburb of Rozelle. I was 23 when we moved into our house, and boy, did we have a lot of work to do!

Just shy of my twenty-fifth birthday, Tristan and I got married. We were well ahead of our group of friends. We were in our mid-twenties and already doing the things that my friends were not even considering at that age, with the house and adult responsibilities that came along with it. We spent our weekends renovating and making a home, while our friends were enjoying their carefree twenties. But we loved nesting and doing what we were doing.

I was still a university student when I was offered a graduate internship with Duty Free Store (DFS) Galleria because of my Japanese language skills. At that time, I was looking for opportunities in the marketing sector, banking on a Japanese boom. My degree was in Communications, but it also touched on marketing, which was what I was interested in. DFS Galleria offered me this opportunity as I was finishing up my course, and I accepted. I worked just as many hours in this management programme as I spent finalising my degree.

But I really didn't enjoy my time, and it wasn't producing the opportunities that I had been promised either. I spent most of my day greeting Japanese tourists in Japanese. It was very tourism-focused, since DFS involved retail with tourists. I was saying the same thing every single day—it was not at all challenging nor did it offer opportunities for learning. So I decided to leave.

I did not have a job to go to, and I had the pressure of a mortgage to pay already. I had never been without a job since I was 15, however I was determined to give myself time to find something that was right for me. It was a couple of weeks of rejection after rejection, as I tried for quite a few different things. That was the first time I had to really look for a job, and it took a while.

MOVING ON UP

I finally found the first real corporate job that fit my skillset after some disappointment and rejection. It was a job advertisement looking for a Japanese-speaking marketing assistant. Perfect!

I went for the job interview at this company, Covance, and Chris, one of my first mentors, interviewed me for the job.

Covance is a clinical research organisation. Pharmaceutical companies outsource their clinical trials to companies like it. They made us do several tests during the interview process. Because of the nature of the work, I had to write and read several papers in Japanese. It was very Japanese-heavy and there was another girl whom they were interviewing as well. Her name was Sylvia and she was Korean, but she was far more fluent in Japanese than I was!

Chris heard my story at length, saw my potential and felt that I was too experienced for the original, junior assistant-level role. With my work ethic, appetite for success and experience in pushing myself to achieve things, I was allowed to skip a level. Chris would become key to my career and professional growth, and I'll always be thankful to him. In the end, they created a new role just for me, while Sylvia got the position that had been advertised.

I worked in Covance for three years, and it was with them that I got my first taste of global travel for business. There I was at the age of 23 in a serious role, before most of my friends in university, while buying my own places to live. My job took me twice to New York in the space of six months. I had never dreamt of going to the United States, but now I found myself there twice over such a short time.

The job also took me to Singapore for the first time. Being exposed to international business and being part of a global marketing team gave me a taste of this bigger world. And being there as a young person made the experience even more dynamic. Everything felt accelerated, and it really hit home that you don't come by these sorts of experiences every day. During my time at Covance, I won a company award and was acknowledged for my marketing skills.

Eventually I started reporting to the Vice President of the region, Lyle, and to this day I'm still in touch with him—another mentor of mine. He also saw the grit and hard work in me, so he was not afraid to give me some truly challenging projects to tackle.

For example, I had helped him put together the expansion strategy for China, India and Taiwan. That involved canvassing the landscape and the market and looking at the right kind of alliance partnerships. I helped determine the value propositions, the market strategy and more. Through him I got my first taste of real strategy as well, which I love to this day.

It helped that I didn't have a nine-to-five mindset, and never minded staying late to finish work. When I was asked to go to a networking event in the evening, or do work after hours, I always treated these occasions as investments in my own career. They were opportunities I knew would never come by again.

Out of recognition for all that work that helped the Asia-Pacific unit, I won my company award, the Bravo Award. Success tasted so sweet because I knew I was building my skillset along with it.

OUR WORST ENEMIES

Not everyone was pleased with my success, and some wanted to pull me down. Our Human Resources manager was one of the nastiest people I'd met, and her behaviour felt like a betrayal of not only myself, but our gender and her profession. No one else at my level and age reported directly to a Vice President, and she was jealous of me and my success. She played up my reporting to a man in his forties as some kind of scandal.

I remember presenting the marketing strategy during a Town Hall Meeting. Many different managers would get up to present, and then it was my turn to give the marketing plans. My face went bright red because I was so nervous presenting in front of the senior leadership. I had already taken it as a learning experience, a point of growth for me—but she then pulled me aside to tell me: "You're going to have to work on that. You were bright as a tomato in there. Going forward, you are going to have to get on top of your presentation skills. You're clearly not ready to be presenting in forums like that."

That was it—no attempt at being constructive or encouraging. She knew how new all this was to me, and it was a calculated, petty move to just tear me down for the sake of it.

Later, I was chosen to come to Singapore to support a medical directors' conference. She objected to me taking the same *flight* as my boss, claiming people would "talk about these things." Never mind that it wasn't just me and him, but many other people coming along. But that kind of pulling down committed by another woman was obvious, and I just could not believe her behaviour.

By that time, I had already experienced a little bit of what it was like being female in a so-called man's world. I had gone to an all-girls' school, and we had a very strong principal who would often tell us that we were getting a good education, and because of it we could do anything. Young, smart, well-educated women could do anything, she told us.

My command of Japanese was also a helpful skill for my employability. By the time I came back from Japan, I was indeed speaking so fluently that I dreamt in Japanese. One of my side jobs in university was as an office assistant with a Japanese paralegal firm that processed immigration visa applications for Japanese people coming to Australia.

To my surprise, despite them knowing that I spoke fluent Japanese and had worked in different jobs before that, they treated me as the tea girl. That was not what I had signed up for—I knew being an office administrative assistant was not going to be a glamorous job, but I certainly knew it was more than just making tea for others.

It was my first taste of people looking down on me despite everything I had to offer. To them, I was nothing more than a foreign tea girl.

What happened to all these things about female empowerment and equal rights? If you have an education, of course you can do the same kind of work and bring just as much to the table. So why do these stereotypes continue to pervade in corporate culture? I was genuinely shocked by that, and had not expected to hit the 'glass ceiling' so early. It was not even a matter of wanting to prove myself; I just felt indignation at the unfairness of it all.

It was not right. And when something doesn't make sense or feel right, I can't go along with it and pretend that it is all okay.

Still, I've to appreciate the irony—the men I worked with were such good mentors and champions of my work and capabilities because they had seen potential in me to nurture, while another woman had chosen to be my worst enemy. I was grateful, I was humble, and I worked hard to demonstrate that their trust was rightly placed in me. My work spoke for itself.

So it broke my heart to tell my boss that I was leaving Covance. He had fought for me and had been such a good mentor, and I knew that leaving would be difficult. But by that point, three years in, I knew I needed a new challenge.

I landed another job soon after that was also instrumental in my career path. (These were the only two big corporate jobs I worked in before I struck out on my own.) This was with a start-up financial management consultancy, targeting CFOs of major Australian companies. I was to be a marketing manager, starting up its marketing function.

I went for a few interviews before I got the job. I was tasked to develop a sample marketing plan and outline a go-to market strategy. It was to my great surprise, and I was not expecting to have a corner office at only 25!

On my first day I was asked to also take on the marketing management role for the more established sister company to the start-up, a global management consulting firm. In other words, I would have responsibility for *both* the more established company and its sister start-up!

Few women worked in the field, and even fewer in high-up positions and demanding jobs like mine. Hours after I began my first day, a colleague came into my office and closed the door. "I'm just going to tell you what I think of marketing, so you can think about it as you start your new job here," he said. "Marketing equals zero value—a big fat zero!"

"We don't value marketing in this company, and I don't know how you're going to change it here," he continued. "Good luck in your job!"

So I began reporting to two MDs and even though it was the MD of the start-up who employed me, and there was that sense of loyalty there, I did find that the work with the management consultancy more challenging and interesting as it was selling to Australia's C-Suite. In the end, after something almost like a tug of war, I chose to dedicate more of my time to the latter.

Some of the men in the company were incredulous that this 'pretty young thing' had come into this senior role, and it grew into a dislike and suspicion of me. The people who hired me, and my bosses, were very complimentary and supportive of me. Both MDs could see that I could match them at an intellectual level, at a maturity level, and at a professional level. I belonged there, and they treated me with respect as they saw what I could contribute.

IT'S A MAN'S WORLD, AND A WOMAN'S GOING TO RULE IT

I had taken on the job of a colleague around my age, which he hated, and he and the others decided then to sort of test me and see what I could do.

In a way, my first-day interloper had been right—marketing wasn't valued much. To my colleagues, it was limited to plying C-suite executives with lavish entertainment and perks, like a corporate box at rugby matches! Everything was macho and domineering, like a competitive sport, and I wanted to do things strategically and differently.

To do that, I would have to run one of the best marketing shows in Australia, and pave the way for thought leadership and credibility in the business-to-business space there. I pushed the region ahead in global recognition, and many of our clients wound up as success stories on the cover of our company magazine.

My boss had the utmost respect for me, and once asked, "Gemma, I want you to go to a networking event in my place. I can't go, will you?" Of course I did, as part of my job was to manage an advisory board of very senior business leaders. Some of them would be there, and the host was Gail Kelly, who would go on to become the CEO of a major Australian bank.

It was a big deal representing our company and being trusted in this high-powered space with our very brand. Of course, the familiar doubts and fears ran through my mind—I was too young, I was a woman, I didn't belong among the who's who. But in those years, despite all of my fears, I would never pass on opportunities like that.

I was riding on a high, but then came the disappointment that eventually led to a change in direction and a new path. Three years into my role, I found out I was pregnant and expecting my first daughter. I was on the plane coming home from a business trip to Auckland watching *March of the Penguins*, a documentary narrated by Morgan Freeman, when I started crying uncontrollably. My colleague was sitting next to me and I was trying to hide the tears, but they kept streaming. I was highly emotional but wasn't sure why. I continued to feel out of sorts over the next week, and so one day I decided to take a pregnancy test—which came back positive. Sure enough, the two blue lines appeared!

Flush with disbelief, I went back into my office, called in a close friend and shared the news with her. I couldn't believe that I was pregnant—it was planned for right then and there.

From that moment forward, my life was about to change in the most positive way, although I didn't realise that at the time. My colleagues began to treat me differently, as if I had suddenly grown two heads overnight. While my body may have been changing, I was still the same Gemma. I still showed up every day, was focused on my work, and still career-driven—surely you can be like that while getting excited about welcoming a little baby into the world?

LOVE WHAT YOU DO

Before I went on maternity leave, my boss and I had spoken about flexible working arrangements when I was ready to come back. He wanted the situation to work for both the company and me. "Gemma, come back when you want and how you want," he said. "We love your work. We love what you do, and you tell me when you are ready to come back."

Sadly, that was not to be. In my six weeks of maternity leave after Charlotte was born, he left the company and I was crushed to hear the news. His replacement was a chauvinistic man who made my life difficult and forced me out of the job.

Once again, it was another reminder that people greatly underestimate women. Just because I'm female and just had a baby, it doesn't mean I can't do my job! In fact, I believe that some of my best results were delivered during those first few months of Charlotte's life. She was such a good baby. She almost knew that I needed to work—not working wasn't an option as I was the breadwinner, and Tristan and I both needed to work.

Charlotte slept well, fed well and was easy-going, so I was still able to manage work commitments and drive these campaigns. Hitting that glass ceiling once again left me with a bitter taste in my mouth. I was in such disbelief. Why couldn't I have a baby and a career when I was making it all work? It was unfathomable because it had been drummed into me as a teenage girl, that I could be anything I wanted to be. No one had told me that I would meet such challenges over and over again, just because I was female.

The work I delivered was excellent throughout, despite my balancing it and motherhood. I even won a global excellence award for my work while I was on maternity leave, but still that wasn't good enough to my new boss.

I did not want to leave Charlotte in day care, and as much as I wanted to play the main part in raising her, I was never going to be a full-time stay-at-home Mum either. I personally need to be mentally and intellectually stimulated, constantly. The mere idea of it sounds like such a foreign concept, as neither my grandmother nor my own mother did that. Tristan and I never even discussed the option. It was impossible due to our mortgage, responsibilities and commitments.

During those months, when I was pregnant and working full-time, I created my first small business on the side, Charlotte's Boutique, selling handcrafted nursery items. And running it gave me a glimpse, a first taste, at what it would be like to run my own thing.

As grating as being pushed out of my job was, there was a silver lining. It was the push I needed to strike out on my own... and in 2008, Manning & Co. was born.

PERSONAL LIFE

Cuddles with Mum. Sydney, January 1980.

Hear me roar! Dressed up as Pebbles from *The Flintstones* at a fancy-dress party in Sydney, February 1982.

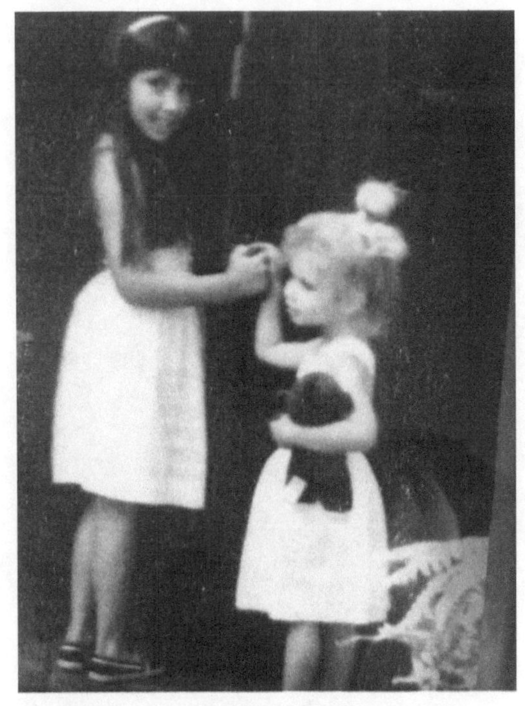

Natalie and me playing in our back garden in Sydney, November 1984. I'm cuddling my trusted friend, Emma the monkey.

Standing on our balcony at our first home in Yorkey's
Knob, Cairns, February 1989. We'd just moved to
Cairns, and it was my first day at the local school.

In Bali learning Balinese dance with my school friends
during our 10-day trip, April 1996. This was my first
time overseas, and a culturally-rich experience that
gave me a lifelong love of travel.

Mum and I hosting my Japanese 'parents' for
afternoon tea, shortly before my wedding in Sydney,
October 2004.

Charlotte and I having afternoon tea with my sister
Natalie in Sydney, December 2008. I had just learnt
that I was expecting Amelie around this time.

Back in Karuizawa, Japan with Charlotte, April 2009.
I was pregnant with Amelie then, and determined to
go while I could still fly. Aichan and I took Charlotte
tandem bike riding, and I'll never forget this special
trip back to Japan.

Dad and me celebrating Charlotte's second birthday in Jubilee Park in Glebe, Sydney, December 2008. Dad's birthday was the day before Charlotte's, and it's always special to celebrate them together.

My first day home from the hospital after Amelie's birth, August 2009. I'm introducing Charlotte to her new baby sister.

Celebrating Mum's 65th birthday in Singapore, at Salt by Luke Mangan, August 2017.

In London to see Kylie Minogue in concert on her Golden Tour, September 2018. It was my second Kylie concert out of Australia!

CHAPTER THREE
DIG DEEP, BACK YOURSELF

I never dreamt about success. I worked for it.

— Estée Lauder

My blood pressure was through the roof from all the stress. "Girls, I don't feel well," I told my daughters Charlotte and Amelie. "I'm just going to the toilet."

I'd barely gotten up when everything went dark. Next thing I knew, I was on the floor, with blood gashing from a head wound and an oxygen mask strapped to my face. I had cracked the back of my head open on an armrest as I went down.

I would have been sent to a hospital, but we were halfway through a flight from Singapore to Sydney. The flight crew and the doctors on board brought me to the back of the plane to examine the extent of my injury, where they bandaged my head and warned me that I would need stitches once we landed.

I did not want Charlotte and Amelie to see what had happened. Thankfully, it was dark on the plane, and they couldn't see the bandage yet. I told them I was fine and to go back to sleep.

It would have been funny in all the absurdity—if it were not just infuriating. No effort was made to help me off the plane after we landed, and despite the searing pain in my head, I still had to get the three of us off the plane on my own. To make matters worse, Amelie (who has motion sickness) had thrown up as we touched down, and I was trying my best to be a courteous passenger and clean her up while holding my head with the other hand. I didn't want Charlotte, who has a phobia of blood, to see the wound—I knew she would be scared and faint.

Somehow, I got my laptop, our coats and bags together, while holding my head still and sealing a bag full of vomit. We all struggled to the customs counter with no help from the crew, and then we faced a long wait to get our passports stamped.

DIG DEEP, BACK YOURSELF

When we finally got to the counter, Charlotte was faint from seeing the blood despite my best efforts. To my dismay, the customs officer insisted on seeing her face to verify her identity! I picked her up and got her to her feet. And with that, after the flight from hell, Australia welcomed me back home.

I didn't want to even think about or know what my flight to Perth, for the opening event of our Innovation Centre, had in store.

PRESSING ON

My disaster of a flight would be just one bump on a very long road. Before that came the birth of my first company, Manning & Co., and its expansion into Asia; my founding of Gemstar and my move to Singapore.

That road began on restless evenings before Charlotte's birth. My first real business, Charlotte's Boutique, came from the need to occupy myself when pregnant with her. I dove right into decorating Charlotte's nursery, but couldn't find what I was after. My evenings were soon spent making my own décor items: I wrapped ribbons around hoops I had purchased from Spotlight. It would form part of an elaborate, two-tier mobile that spelt out Charlotte's name. I then spent evening upon evening crafting matching items that decorated every inch of the nursery.

After Charlotte was born, I joined a local mothers' group as most new mothers do, and for that first year, the mums would often get together and go to each other's houses. The other mums loved the items I'd made, and that was how Charlotte's Boutique was born. My maternity leave, much like the entirety of the pregnancy, was not a time for me to kick back—that is not in my nature. I've always loved to be busy. So I ramped up production and laid the groundwork for the business, visiting suppliers and selling my products in markets.

It was not a particularly long maternity leave, but when I returned to the office, I realised how much I missed doing more intellectually stimulating work. The taste of operating my own business was tantalising, but I wanted to do more. Business strategy ignites me, and retail did not.

Fortunately, my new boss was less than understanding of my desire to be a present mother while being a career-driven woman. I say fortunately, because if he had not made it difficult for me to stay in my role, I might not be writing this book. His old-fashioned views made it impossible to work beside him. And with a consulting job offer from my previous boss, who had found out what was going on, I knew that my corporate career was over—and that a new adventure was waiting.

It happened relatively quickly. I had just about a week to set everything up, so I secured working space in a warehouse building near my home in Balmain, registered Manning & Co., recruited an assistant, and began working with my first client—a Brisbane-based telecommunications company.

The demands kicked in immediately. I was flying to Brisbane every fortnight, staying a few days each time. Tristan, my then-husband, was working four-day weeks so he had at least one full day to take care of Charlotte, while my mum helped whenever she could around her own business. Charlotte herself was a very good baby, and it was almost as if she already knew what was at stake and she simply worked with our schedule. I was very lucky to have the kind of support I did, because I leapt right into business and loved it. When you are in the thick of it, you don't get the chance to stop and think if you can balance it all. You just do.

But as life goes, problems started emerging. I was providing full-service marketing consulting services for the telco in Brisbane—brand positioning, competitor analysis, brand messaging, developing the go-to-market strategy. etc. My former boss served as its MD, and I enjoyed working with him again.

I was grateful for the opportunity, but my client's business encountered cash flow problems and I was one of the suppliers they couldn't pay. So in the first six months into my new business, I experienced my first challenge as a business owner. I wasn't paid for several of my invoices, and on hindsight, it was a good learning experience for a new entrepreneur. It was a steep learning curve, yes, but from it I learnt the importance of contracts, documenting everything and negotiation.

When you work in a service-based business, there are a lot of variables in play, and you need to have the right fundamentals in place while knowing how to pivot when things go wrong. Six months into business, I was engaging a solicitor to claw back some of the monies owed to me. I had success, but owed the solicitor half of my income from them. (That company is no longer around.)

Word got out among my former colleagues and corporate network that I was running my own consulting business. From a very solid business network that I had established in my earlier corporate life, I gained new clients immediately—enough to keep me busy and grow my team. I didn't have to go out and hunt for clients, because they came to me. I even secured clientele from the mothers' group I was involved in.

My excellent business network provided the core of my company's early success. By the third year I was shortlisted for the *Telstra Young Businesswoman of the Year* award, unfortunately losing out to well-known entrepreneur Jodie Fox—who won for her business Shoes of Prey, which she successfully expanded to the US. Unfortunately, it's no longer around.

Two and a half years on, my growing team was preparing to move out of that co-working space. I was securing a new lease for bigger premises when I found out that I was pregnant once again. Talk about timing! I was so worried about taking on my own lease at this stage as there were so many unknowns. How would I manage this fast-growth business *and* welcome my second baby into the world?

Like Charlotte, Amelie was a complete surprise. But I think we were all the better for it because that would have been the only way I could have managed it all and still had the family I wanted. I dived into the deep end, and rolled with the punches.

Amelie, a Leo-child, was born with a wild roar. She was such a happy, cute baby, but proved to be fussier than Charlotte. It was her way or the highway from the very start! She didn't fit into my busy working schedule as much as Charlotte had. By the time she was born, the business was already in full swing—and growing more quickly than I imagined.

This time around, I worked even while going into labour. Days before releasing a major report for a client, I was doing some last-minute adjustments when my contractions started. "I'm so sorry, but I've started contractions," I wrote in an email to them. "I'm going into labour! Everything is under control, and I will be in touch soon with an update!"

It was an intense period juggling a toddler, a young baby and a rapidly growing business. There was no way to take time off, and during this time I slept little and suffered from breast inflammation (mastitis) five times. Amelie wasn't a good sleeper, and I had to meet the needs of a toddler who was trying to grasp the fact that she now had a little sister in the world.

But I insisted on being an active and involved mum and a businesswoman. I didn't want to miss out on my girls. Instead, I wanted to afford them the full experience of having an involved mother, while not setting my own dreams aside.

In a way, it would have been nice to not have worked in those early years and just focused on being a mother. But I knew that my business was going places, and had some amazing opportunities for our future—and did not want to lose that.

Through it all, I couldn't cut corners. I've never wanted to outsource the parenting of my girls and I continue to be present, involved and interested in them. They are my best friends, and my everything.

SINGAPORE CALLING

Manning & Co. was started during the 2008 financial crisis. As lots of businesses were going under, we thrived. From 2008 to 2012, we had year-on-year growth and excellent cash flow. I ran a lean machine and invested back into the business, so I kept my earnings rather minimal.

But things are cyclical in the world of business, and soon we hit a bit of a road bump. On the back of Australia's mining bust, every sector was suffering the impact of a slowdown. Clients started to pull back on their marketing expenditures, and so we had to shrink and scale back.

Worse, I was separating from Tristan and thus, had to take on more financial responsibility. Before all this though, a big opportunity landed on my lap.

Newport Consulting was instrumental in the growth of Manning & Co., and they were among our bigger clients. They were doing well in Australia in those years, and expanding into other markets. Wherever Newport went, so did Manning & Co., and I had the good fortune of travelling to South Africa and London for their business. I count their founder and CEO, David Hand, amongst my mentors—he was a key factor in my company's success, and remains a dear friend of mine. Without his belief in me and my company, we would not have gotten to where we are now. For that, I will always be indebted to Dave.

When Newport was looking to expand into Southeast Asia, he turned to us as the company to bring them in. We essentially entered Singapore together, despite the presence of established competitors on the ground. He had that much faith in us since we had a great working relationship, and I was familiar with the ins-and-outs of his business.

We were launching a big thought leadership event, centred on operational excellence, over two days at the iconic Raffles Hotel. Featuring expert speakers and attendees from across the region, it sold many tickets and was a huge success that pleased both of us. In the run up to the event, I networked with all sorts of different people, and was connected to the Australian business community in Singapore.

I believe in nurturing relationships, and networking is definitely key to business success. Not just for the sake of selling, but to genuinely build rapport and relationships. So it is through this experience that I began to connect the dots and see an opportunity, a niche that we could occupy.

We were getting lots of tech start-ups coming to Manning & Co. for strategic marketing advice. By way of evolution, between 70 and 80 percent of our clientele is in the technology and IT world, so it was only natural that we were being recommended to start-ups. Australia then did not have the right infrastructure to support the growth of this sector, and we were experiencing a brain drain of tech entrepreneurs moving to California's Silicon Valley—instead of growing their businesses in Australia.

All the time I had been spending in Singapore lent me the opportunity to become well-versed in how the business world operates here. And fortuitously, right around this time Singapore had just announced its Smart Nation plan, offering robust funding to entrepreneurs and the right infrastructure for them to set up.

Singapore was determined to be the Silicon Valley of the East. There was my opportunity… and how Gemstar came to be.

FINDING FOOTING

I don't like remaining stagnant. In the early years of my corporate career, I never spent more than three years in one company. By the time Gemstar was born, I had already been running Manning & Co. for five years, so it was time for a new challenge. It didn't mean I was setting it aside—rather, I was growing an ecosystem and Gemstar was a side project that grew as I kept connecting the dots and finding solutions to problems that I had identified through all the networking I did, travelling back and forth between Australia and Singapore.

My name soon became known in the tech world as the go-between. We were being associated with tech and innovation while in Australia, and then as the go-to for Australian start-ups while in Singapore. The National Research Foundation (NRF) reached out to us in 2015 saying that they wanted to do an Australian Pavilion centred on tech for the first time. Back then it was called Tech Venture, and it was one of the region's biggest conferences, bringing tech companies and venture capitalists together. It was *the* place to get tech deals done in the region. We were asked to represent Australia for the first time ever—the US and the UK had always been showcased, but not Australia.

I brought five companies to showcase at the Tech Venture Conference. At the same time, we were hosting immersion programmes bringing these companies into Singapore, on a full week's programme hosting networking lunches, targeted one-on-one meetings and pitches, and cocktails in the evening. Our programmes were focused on networks, relationships and showing our companies what they need to achieve when dipping their toes into Asia.

Through all this work, Gemstar became instrumental in lobbying for Australian companies to prioritise Southeast Asia in their growth plans. We were not the first to carve out a space in the Australian market as a kind of gateway into Asia, but I'd say we certainly made a big impact in educating and warming up Australian businesses to think ASEAN. We were quoted in the media several times due to our work and at this stage, I was still doing all of this from Sydney.

Moving physically to Singapore was one of my riskiest and most courageous moves. I had not planned on moving initially, but building on the momentum of success with Gemstar, I felt that this was the next step and the only way that I was going to be successful in my business expansion. I was going to set up an Innovation Centre, with the strategy of creating a landing pad for companies needing to get a foothold in the region.

The focus was to be an end-to-end market entry and growth partner for Australian companies. When our clients sign up and become a part of Gemstar, they have a physical place within this Innovation Centre in Singapore to operate out of—a perfect solution for any Australian company looking to establish itself in this market. We provide all the necessary services available to them as well as networks and introductions. Since Singapore is a hyper-competitive market with red tape from the government to navigate, Gemstar is their acceleration and gateway.

It was a huge undertaking for me, and a new milestone in my entrepreneurial journey. Up to this point, I wouldn't really have classified myself an entrepreneur. (You see, the word comes from the French term *entreprendre*, which means 'to undertake'.) Although I created M&C from scratch and built that business from the bottom up, expanding my business to Singapore was definitely the riskiest move I had made at that stage in business.

I had to re-mortgage my house to fund the expansion and opening of the Innovation Centre and all the other set-up costs, including my first Singapore hire. I always think people who are serious about their businesses are willing to back themselves, and put their money where their mouth is. I was to be taken seriously in my business expansion and putting it all on the line.

And then several things started going awry. The four businesses which had agreed to sign into my Innovation Centre, which would have guaranteed my revenue and covered my costs, fell through—almost all at once. I had already signed my lease and had everything set up. Nothing went right in that initial period. My strength and resilience were tested every day, and several of the start-ups that did work with us never paid their invoices. It was a trying time and a learning experience too, with the risks involved in working with start-ups.

At the same time, the *Australian government* itself started to focus on the funding and start-up issues in Australia, and announced its Austrade initiative. Five landing pads around the world were set up to help Aussie start-ups expand internationally. Funding from the government would allow chosen start-ups to join these programmes for 90 days, and it was all fully funded. Guess which country was among the five chosen?

Now Gemstar had been one of the active voices in persuading the government about Singapore's value in the growth plans of Australian start-ups. We were newly incorporated and bringing Australian start-ups into Singapore—and now the government had decided to do it all for free!

In the course of building my connections and business in Singapore, I had a lot of conversations with various stakeholders including several government organisations, with a view to collaborate. Now I was a competitor, and there were lots of shades of grey. I witnessed all the underhanded dealings first-hand, and came away disillusioned and deflated. I had experienced bullish behaviour and the dirty game of politics at a whole new level.

On top of all of that, I had to deal with the direct impact of my decision to move to Singapore on the people around me. Unlike many expats who have school fees included in their packages, I was moving for my own business. After having borrowed money to fund the expansion, how was I going to afford life in Singapore and come up with the $80,000 or so to put my girls into international schools? The economics of moving to Singapore delayed the move by at least six months or so.

By the time we finally moved to Singapore, I had found a temporary solution. I enrolled the girls in distance education—they would finish the school year while still enrolled in a school in Sydney, and do all of their education via online learning. I recall being at an exclusive event at the Australian High Commissioner's residence, talking in a crowd of people and someone asking what international school I was sending my girls to. I replied that I wasn't and that they were being homeschooled instead. There was an awkward silence that followed—not quite the reaction that the group of people were expecting.

So for the first nine months or so, the girls were effectively homeschooled—just to add to the stressors from my business adding to my increasing blood pressure. It compounded with the stress of an increased mortgage; things not going to plan and the government entering as a competitor; moving to another country; and running my teams and clients in Australia where we had just had turmoil over staff changeover.

RESILIENCE

I had learnt a lot about resilience by my thirties, much of it from just watching Mum as I grew up. My mum has bucketloads of inner strength and resilience, but at the time I didn't really know much about it, other than her being brave and courageous.

I know plenty of men in business who leave their families at home to pursue their entrepreneurial dreams or careers in Singapore. They have been able to establish themselves here and kick things off, then move their families across later or just visit home regularly.

I could not do that as a single mother; there was no option to leave the girls in Sydney and base myself in Singapore. I had been feeling sick to my core since before the move. How the hell was I going to do this?

What have I done? I've created a monster! I thought.

For weeks leading up to the move, I couldn't sleep. Instead, I paced the house in the small hours over all the decisions I had to make. I wanted to achieve what I had set out to do, and I had already financially invested so much. Yet I felt incredibly challenged and guilty over the reality of uprooting the girls and taking them away from Tristan and their family.

Tristan and I had divorced by this point. We had been together since I was 17, and achieved so many milestones together—buying our first apartment and then house, making two renovations, travelling and most importantly, having two beautiful girls together. All of this while many of our friends our age were still finding their way around life.

Yet we had grown apart, as many couples do when they get together so young. Tristan and I separated when I was 32, and divorced a few years later. Tristan remains a dedicated, doting and loving father, and while I don't think we were meant to be romantically together for life's full journey, we *were* destined to be good friends for life—and that is what we are today.

There were some steep learnings surrounding our parting ways, especially after spending half of our life together. I learnt that life is not black and white, and that there are many shades of grey. I also came to terms with the fact that you can't control everything in life, as much as I like to be in control! That sometimes while things don't make sense in your head, they make sense in your heart, and sometimes you have to lead with the heart. I lead with my heart in all that I do, whether that is business, or in my personal life. Sometimes, it is a good thing and sometimes it isn't, but I wouldn't change this part of who I am.

Towards the end of 2017, I was pretty much at breaking point with all the immense stress I was under. There is only so much one can physically and mentally take. I had seen Mum go through periods of immense turmoil during her time in business. I didn't really understand it, until the risks were higher for me and I started to take more risks—and more pressure as a result. Besides the move to Singapore and all the difficulties I faced, I was unnerved by the dirty tactics of so many around me.

It was all too much, and the following year proved to be even worse. My girls kept me going through all of this—they always do. At the root of my resilience, grit and inner strength was also my dogged determination to not let anyone tell me that I can't do something, that I wouldn't make it or that something was impossible. The naysayers fuel my drive even more.

The plans I had for Gemstar at the time were not working out. Competition was fierce and ruthless, and I was starting to not enjoy working with start-ups. Start-ups are high-risk and have a very different mentality from SMEs or our M&C multinational clients, who understand the concept of paying fees for services. When I started my business and was essentially in start-up mode, I would never think about not paying rent, or invoices for services. I could not quite understand the new start-up mentality that had emerged in newer businesses. Many of them, I would find out, expected those things for free! There is even a real mind-set and culture around this behaviour.

Thus, I decided to pivot slightly. Agility and mobility are things that I believe sound businesses and leaders master. Things are always changing, and you can't be too fixed in business.

That was when I created YoungGems®. I was approached to teach entrepreneurship to young people, and that was whom this programme was initially for. It came at a time when I wanted to add more diversity to the Gemstar business. By this point we were inviting, based on trust, between 50 to 100 people to meet companies we were showcasing under Gemstar in Singapore. It was like being constantly swarmed by sharks though—everyone was trying to sell their own services which were overlapping with Gemstar, even as they were there to drink our wine, eat our food and meet our clients. Everyone was wanting to make a buck under my dime, and I found it all slimy and horrible. To make things worse, I was often mistaken as the Event Manager at our events, with people mistaking any males I had working with me at the time as the 'Boss'. I stopped enjoying the innovative environment of the start-up world, and getting into education was a new challenge.

We created YoungGems® IP, building on what we do in Gemstar and Manning & Co., by teaching people how to grow their business ideas and solve real world problems. Our YoungGems® programmes delivered amazing results and when a global higher education institute attended one of our pitch events, they were so impressed with what they saw that they asked us if we wanted to do a diploma course with them.

In the meantime, a string of events happened that truly tested my resilience—I had what seemed like a constant battle on my hands. Each time I pushed the boundaries and went out of my own comfort zone, the mountains appeared that much higher to climb. It felt like I always had to have my boxing gloves on, and watch my back too.

When I expanded into Perth, Western Australia, barely a year after moving to Singapore, once again things didn't go according to plan, despite the positive signals and opportunities that were presented to me. We were doing the YoungGems® programme with a university in Singapore and Perth at the time, and our partners floated the idea of an Innovation Centre in Perth, which their students could use as an off-campus lab. Despite conversations about partnering with us, that university went ahead and opened its own similar centre and decided to partner with others. Around the same time, I was approached by an investor/businessman through a mutual contact, and he was very keen for me to open that very facility in Perth!

He offered one of his commercial properties to be the headquarters for our programmes in WA and wanted to invest in a pipeline of tech companies that we would bring into this space. I was not planning on expanding into Perth right then and there, seeing as I was still trying to stabilise things in Singapore, which I had only recently opened. But all these things coming together seemed ripe for another expansion.

Negotiations took place during Christmas time, and there was a lot of pressure from him to get the deal done. My accountant was on holiday, and so were most people since it was Christmas. When I did put forth figures, which my advisors and I thought was a reasonable partnership arrangement, he showed his true colours. From deferring to my terms as I was assuming so much more risk than he was, he now demanded at least half ownership of the venture—despite the agreement that it was up to me as to what I would feel was a fair arrangement. The property market in Perth is incredibly flat, so he was only offering real estate while we would be bringing in all the IP, expertise and relationships needed.

Despite this, and my reasonable offer, he did not budge, and I trusted my gut instinct. I was not going to be bullied into something that I wasn't comfortable with. We found a far more competitive space in the end, at a fraction of the cost. Still, it was a large undertaking and there were still Singapore and Sydney to contend with. My forecasts were to fund the Perth expansion through cash flow, and our joint venture around the Diploma was a key part of it.

With the Diploma not coming through when we expected, it put further strain on the business and created more headaches culminating in a great deal of personal stress and anxiety. Now I had Perth overheads to address, as well as an increasing payroll too. Business isn't based on textbook theory—in the real world things don't always go to plan and again, it is how you respond as a business leader that is key. The sleepless nights were countless.

In the build-up to our opening in Perth, we were approached to be one of the key players in a hackathon event and contribute by hosting the event. We had the opportunity to boost our profile by hosting it, as well as bring forward our Singapore connections and Asia engagement proposition too.

However, we ran into even more underhanded politics, and it was clear that the advisory committee did not want us involved. We were in competition with another main player, and they did everything they could to milk our knowledge as sponsors, while locking us out of anything that could benefit us. We suddenly realised what a closed market WA was and if you were entering in from the outside, you were a target. Especially me—not only was I based in Asia, but I was originally from Sydney, the evil East Coast of Australia.

Our initial contact who introduced this opportunity to us couldn't do anything, and suddenly disappeared. We were thrown into the lion's den.

Yet little did they know that by removing us as hosts, our Singapore contacts would ask questions and their own credibility would come under fire, which was what ended up happening.

All of this, and we were just about to open our doors! That brings us to the ill-fated flight that opens this chapter, and wonderfully encapsulates all the problems I was facing.

I had my head glued together in Sydney, and then took a domestic flight to Perth to carry on with our opening event. To add salt to an already extremely sore wound, the Guest of Honour to the event walked straight up to Phil, my male non-executive director. "Oh, it's so nice to meet you," he said. "What inspired you? What motivated you to open up Gemstar in Perth?"

Phil deftly steered him to me and introduced us properly, making it clear that I am the Founder and CEO of Gemstar. But that was not the end of it. I found out that very night that the Advisory Committee for the hackathon event had essentially backstabbed us by going with our competitor, despite them agreeing to use a non-competitor's venue for the event. I had to get through the rest of the night—a milestone event and what should have been one of celebration and cheer—with a wounded head and a very sore back, all the while keeping a smile on my face.

When you are the face of a company, the brand ambassador and founder, you have to be an actor in many ways. You often have to perform, switching it on and off. You have to carry yourself in front of so many, without letting anyone see the pain, disappointment and hurt that sometimes is on the inside.

It was this way during my divorce too, when the show had to keep going on. I often wanted nothing more than to crawl into a ball and hide myself away from the business world, and just deal with my own turmoil instead of everything else. But no, the show must go on.

NO OTHER WAY BUT ONWARD AND UPWARD

I get deeply disappointed with people in business. I don't mean to generalise, and I've come across a lot of great people too, don't get me wrong. However, overall, I've come across a lot of people who don't operate the way I do; I expect that they will, but many times I've seen that isn't the case.

There are so many unethical people and organisations, who don't conduct themselves professionally. I've been doing this for 12 years and I'm still appalled by the behaviour that I come up against, and it takes every bit of strength and determination in me to keep on going and get past it.

During this period, I was approached by another state government in Australia to outline a programme based on our work at Gemstar to take start-ups into India and set up a Gemstar Innovation Centre of Excellence there. I was asked to put a detailed proposal and budget together and outline my approach for such a programme. I would have to act quickly, as it needed to be announced and kicked off in only a short time. It took me weeks to pull the strategy together—talking to partners, working through the details, etc. We understood that Gemstar would run it, but the state government suddenly changed their plans, opening up the process and inviting other companies to put forward their tenders.

My proposal still hit the mark and delivered what they were looking for. But to my total surprise, they used it to shape the tender process... and awarded the project to someone else!

That a government had the audacity to behave like this was another deep shock. All my ideas and expertise would now benefit a competitor, and this happening during my two years of hell almost tipped me over the edge. It was part of a long run of bad luck, but it taught me not to trust promises too readily, whoever made them.

So many times, people have gone out of their way to see me fail. Maybe it is because I'm a mover and shaker. A visionary who can see things before others, and someone who can execute and make things happen. While you might say business is indeed a cutthroat world, does it have to be? I don't think so.

After several years of extending myself, pushing the boundaries, taking risks and things not going to plan almost leading to a breakdown, business started to settle and turn around in 2019.

I won a social impact project in partnership with AccessPlus, a Western Australia organisation supporting the deaf community. The opportunity was to teach entrepreneurship to the deaf and hard of hearing there, at a time when I had lost confidence and faith in the WA market—and the 'cowboy' business practices I had experienced, especially in the innovation sector.

The uncanny thing here is that unbeknownst to me at the time, my beloved grandmother (my Big Nanny), had been involved with the deaf and hard of hearing community. She had employed the deaf in her manufacturing business in the 1950s at a time when it was unheard of to employ deaf (or back then the deaf and dumb) people. When I told Mum that I had won this project, she teared up and said, "Gemma, you are so much like your grandmother." When I opened our programme in Perth later that year, I was extremely emotional. I had goosebumps as I signed up our first cohort. I felt like my grandmother was there in the room with me smiling at me.

My mum flew from Sydney to Perth to join me for the pitch event and see my work in action. I know she was super proud of me, and in disbelief about the similarities between me and my grandmother.

This was a turning point. We saw a series of several new project wins and growth in Singapore and Perth, for both businesses. It has taken me five years since I started expanding Manning & Co., in Asia to get to this point. One of our key teachings to companies wanting to expand into Asia is that it takes time and requires great patience—my own business is proof of this.

My Singapore business has now outperformed my Australian business, and we are turning a profit. We experienced strong year-on-year growth, and it has taken five years of hard work, investing a ton of time, money, and energy (and blood and sweat!) to get to this point. Sometimes, the companies that we come across want it all to happen overnight. But from my experience, it takes a whole lot more to get to the point of success in Asia.

I recently celebrated my fortieth birthday in Singapore. It meant so much to me to celebrate a milestone birthday in a country that has been so instrumental in my journey. The decade leading up to it was huge—everything you can possibly imagine thrown into it. It was a coming of age in many ways, and involved lots of change. Divorce, creating a second business, moving to a new country... the list goes on. It all forced me to grow, teaching me resilience and showing me how important it is to have the right people around you—personally and professionally. Looking back on it all now, I wonder how I managed to keep on going despite all the obstacles, setbacks, and challenges.

My daughters both have big dreams and I always tell them, "Girls, I've dreamt big." I dreamt of building a business in another country against all odds, when everything seemed impossible financially. I dreamt big then and I'm still dreaming big, and I want to show my girls that you need to put the work in to achieve your dreams. Nobody is going to hand them to you, and sometimes it takes years and years to see it all come to fruition. Sometimes a snowball of disasters will make you question why you chose it in the first place. But that is all part of the journey.

I think people are surprised at how far I've come, especially in Singapore where so many tried to muscle me out initially, with all smiles of course. I doubt that the powers that be would have thought that this petite young woman could follow through, uproot and physically move to Singapore to execute her plan, and still be standing. It's almost like I had climbed a mountain that many people have failed to, and many more didn't believe I could.

We have seen a lot of men eyeing this market, wanting to bring something similar up here but never being able to do it on their own terms. They have formed alliances and partnerships, only to disappear just as quickly. But here I am, doing it all without any grants or outside funding.

So I think part of turning 40 and celebrating it in Singapore is also about sending a message to my critics and the naysayers. I'm immensely proud of what has been achieved, what I'm celebrating and the fact that my business is growing. If I had to return to Australia tomorrow, I know I can do it after achieving what I set out to do.

CHAPTER FOUR
LEAD WITH COURAGE

LEAD WITH COURAGE

> Fearlessness is not the absence of fear. It's the
> mastery of fear. It's about getting up one more
> time than we fall down.
>
> — Arianna Huffington

Would you believe me if I told you that I was dancing on table tops in the Caribbean next to Sir Richard Branson, besides dining next to flamingos, racing boats, hugging lemurs and zip lining across the island—all for work? Necker Island was definitely one of the highlights of my entrepreneurship journey; the bright light in an otherwise arduous journey that tested my mettle to the utmost.

Integrity is such a core value of mine, even with all the sliminess that I've experienced in business. I can't be any different from what I am inside, and despite my shock and disappointment, I've gone on without throwing in the towel or worse, stooping to their level.

Integrity, responsibility, and accountability are the qualities I promote in business with my team. Through my journey, I've always been accountable, responsible, and unafraid to keep being that way. Business owners obviously have accountability to different stakeholders, employees, shareholders, and so on. But I think just taking accountability for your own work and having responsibility for it is something that is so important and that I strongly encourage.

I don't always see it in other people. But when I look back on my own upbringing and remember the hardworking people around me, It reminds me what has shaped me and my approach to business.

Another important value I strive to promote in business is diversity. Being able to embrace diversity and respect others' differences is important, especially as we grow as a business internationally. We are a global business now, not just a Singaporean or an Australian one. And this all comes back to my very strong drive for an equal playing field.

The very first time that I became aware of inequality was when I was 10 years old in Year Five. There was an end of year excellence award, and it was assumed that girls could not win it. The teacher even said to my class: "Boys, don't forget the end of year excellence award coming up. You need to work hard for it."

Imagine that—addressing only the boys, ignoring the girls who made up the other half of the class! There was a clear bias against girls, and I wasn't going to settle for it. That was also the first time I refused to accept the status quo.

It gave me the motivation to work really hard that year on my times tables and reading. I did everything that I could to help me get the award, and I succeeded. My mum and I still laugh about it because I still have the book that I won. It was by Banjo Paterson, a famous Australian poet, and it sits proudly on my bookshelf.

It was not really about the award, but the principle of it. I was not going to let somebody tell me that I could not do something or achieve a goal because I was only a girl. And it was not about me specifically, but about the group I was automatically put into. Every day since then, I have fought against this bias of what I can or can't do based on my gender. Be it in that Japanese paralegal firm; my pregnancy with Charlotte when I was suddenly viewed as an alien with two heads; or that incident where my non-executive director was simply assumed to be the owner of Gemstar, I've had to work harder for what I've achieved because of my gender. Creating a level playing field, whether it's gender, age, ethnicity, or being disadvantaged, is crucial—not just for me, but for future generations.

I started out my business when I was younger than most, and people discounted me early on. But even if young people don't know everything, why not give an opportunity to those with the right mindset and attitude? Why not guide and encourage them?

Part of my frustration is the realisation that my path would have likely been a lot easier had I been a man. But I don't dwell on this—instead, I'm driven more to make positive and impactful change through my own actions and efforts.

I spent Australia Day 2015 at King George Island in Antarctica. Travelling to Antarctica is up there with some of the most memorable experiences I've ever had. It was a tough decision to go—I had been invited to participate in an entrepreneur's think tank there, but it coincided with my youngest daughter Amelie starting her first year at kindergarten.

I was torn. Should I go to that life-changing opportunity, despite knowing I would miss Amelie's first day at school? My mum assured me that Amelie would forgive me—besides, there would be so many other first events in her life. The irony is that Amelie still reminds me all these years later that I missed her first day at school!

As you can imagine, I was talk of the school at the time—the mum who missed her daughter's first day of school. I remember being on the icebreaker and trying to call Amelie before she took off for school. Calling ship to shore was difficult and expensive, and a fellow Aussie entrepreneur saw me break down at the concierge in tears when I couldn't get through and talk to Amelie on her special day. He kindly gave me the few hundred dollars needed to finally make the seconds-long call!

But I'm glad I went. For 10 days, we discussed collaboration, co-creation, and creative thinking, with the aim to create new ventures among some of Australia's most promising entrepreneurs. There were people from all over Australia, networking and pitching ideas to one another. Someone connected me to another entrepreneur who ran a successful incubator in Sydney, but didn't have an Asian presence; Gemstar might be a good solution and collaboration.

At every meal you could sit wherever you wanted, so you'd sit next to a different person every day. It was pretty surreal to have an iceberg float by while you were talking to people!

I found one of my venture capitalist lunch partners standoffish, even aggressive. Still, I kept being pleasant and decided to share some of my work in Asia. But as I was speaking, he literally turned his back to me and talked to his VC mate next to him! I'd encountered rudeness before, but this was at another level.

There were not many women in attendance at this think tank. We were 100 people in all, with only some 20 or 30 women... but *all* of them had something to say about this person's aggressive behaviour and rudeness. Some were horrified that he worked in an industry that could make or break people's dreams.

Worse, he was so rude and arrogant that he reduced some of the younger women to tears when they went to pitch their ideas to a panel that he was sitting on. Even an older woman, who was one of Australia's original angel investors and had set up the community, was very put off by him.

It's one thing to agree on one man's bad attitude, but another to realise that men like him are sadly common in the start-up and VC scenes. They are responsible for so many people's future dreams, and while there might have been some progression since then, there is still nowhere near enough diversity among VCs. The ones I've come across are largely arrogant, rude and military-like, crushing people's dreams every day.

A year or so later, I crossed paths with him again as he was presenting at one of my clients' boardroom events. Ironically, he had just launched an initiative celebrating young female entrepreneurs, simply because he had cottoned on to the fact that young female entrepreneurship was becoming a thing in Australia. The hypocrisy of it! This known chauvinist was now pivoting to offer accolades just because he smelled an opportunity.

Seeing what such people do irritates me to no end, because there is neither substance nor authenticity to their actions. This isn't an isolated example either, and I've seen acts like this many times along the way.

That boorish behaviour didn't spoil my trip. I was making friends for life and doing incredible things, from drinking whisky with 10,000-year-old ice to climbing glaciers, walking down ice mountains with penguins, cruising past massive icebergs and physically passing the South Pole.

It was a trip of a lifetime on all fronts, and his behaviour didn't put a damper on all the things I learnt from it. Antarctica was an amazing opportunity and buoyed by that experience, I jumped right back into the fray and steered my ship deftly through stormy weather.

And my resilience and adaptability bore fruit. Over the last few years, the businesses have received some wonderful recognition from the industry and my peers. I'm most proud of the *Entrepreneur of the Year* award I won in 2018, because I received it when everything around me was crumbling. Not that many people around me knew what I was really going through, and there I was being recognised for my achievements despite it all. We were also listed as a *Global 100* company last year, and recognised as the *Best Marketing and PR company* in 2019 by APAC Insider and *Best Marketing and PR* company in Asia 2019 and 2020 by ACQ5. And this year we were called out as one of the top 85 PR firms in the world, and the only one in Asia, by Forrester's assessment of PR companies for the IT sector. These awards have brought validation to all our hard work and sacrifices during the grind.

LIFE LESSONS FROM SIR RICHARD BRANSON

Keep to your values, and do the work needed long enough... and it will not just be awards you will score.

Through a chain of events, I was fortunate enough to meet one of my life-long heroes, Sir Richard Branson. One of my friends from the Antarctica trip had heard me talk about the social impact venture that I wanted to launch next. He had been invited to Branson's private estate on Necker Island, and met Branson before.

He put my name forward for the next such gathering. "Let me get you an interview to see if you can get through," he told me.

You had to go through a process of talking to the organiser, who is very close to Branson. It's an invitation-only kind of opportunity;

Antarctica was already an amazing experience and then to follow that up with meeting Branson at Necker the next year was unbelievable.

A week on Necker Island is one spent with Branson in person the whole time. You can have every meal with him if you want! I remember being star-struck at first. It was so surreal—here I was in the British Virgin Islands, one of the most magical places on earth, at Branson's private island and home. It was also the knowledge that I was in the same place where he had hosted famous world leaders, like Nelson Mandela and Barack Obama.

Necker is famous for its temple library, where global leaders have discussed matters of international importance. And that was where I first revealed my social impact business idea, Light Years.

I was fortunate to spend some quality time with him. We were seated together at some meals, and discussed gender diversity, equality and entrepreneurship. I've since kept in touch with him about the different things I'm doing, and since meeting him, I've developed the YoungGems® Programme even more. It's since become a diploma in Singapore, and at its launch the books we gave the students were personally autographed by him.

Branson is one of my entrepreneurial heroes, because I find his story to be absolutely incredible. He has faced adversity, being dyslexic and dropping out of school. I like that he exemplifies entrepreneurial traits like resilience and grit, taking risks, having courage and challenging the status quo. You don't need to go to university for that. (Yes, I went to university myself, but I don't think that you need multiple degrees to be a success in life.)

Many people still pursue diplomas and advise their children on their career paths, while still being unsure about what their own future careers will look like. But the world has changed very quickly, and it's become clear that you don't need to rely on the traditional pathway of going to university for future success.

That was one thing I learnt from Branson. Entrepreneurship arms you with the resources you need to succeed in this world, whether that is for running your own business or being a problem-solver in any environment. He is always curious, questioning things and trying to solve problems, and I admire that trait. He has entered and disrupted whole industries because of this quality. In a way, I've done the same. My inquisitive mind has led me to wanting to solve problems, and along the way I can disrupt the status quo—not something people are always comfortable with.

Being inquisitive, asking the tough questions and challenging the norms are all things we encourage and teach in our YoungGems® entrepreneurship programme. More than anything, I think we need business-mindedness more than the bog-standard degrees coming out of the universities. Branson and I are aligned in our thinking.

On Necker, I was with 30 people from around the world. I also made friends for life during my time there. I engaged in once-in-a-lifetime business conversations, and had the opportunity to build unique global networks, deepen relationships and discuss ideas with Branson himself. On top of this, we remembered to have fun, sailing, dancing and zip-lining. Being with like-minded game changers ignites me. I get so much from it and it helps feed my motivation, energy and drive.

It was life-changing. Necker helped shape my future, and opened my eyes to all kind of possibilities and ventures. That's what I want to do for our YoungGems® students—to help open their eyes and to think more globally, and not just restrict themselves to their domestic market. Singapore may be strategic, but it's small and that lack of size can constrict our business thinking. The same goes for Australia in many ways, and we need to open up.

WORK LIFE

Me during the early years of Manning & Co. in Sydney, March 2010. I had an office in the basement level, beneath the shop fronts on Darling Street. The office was conveniently a five-minute drive from home, and close to the school that the girls eventually went to.

With some of my team at a special Christmas function for clients in Sydney, December 2012. Manning & Co. has always considered its clients like family.

Singapore, September 2016. In the first few years of Gemstar, we would regularly conduct immersion programmes that linked Australian companies with our Singapore network. Here I introduce our visiting delegation of companies with my business mentor, Non-Executive Director and friend, Phil Forrest, by my side.

In Antarctica, February 2015. It was the trip of a lifetime, and I'll never forget its beauty or the people I shared the experience with.

With Sir Richard Branson on Necker Island, June 2016.
It was incredibly special to share a moment with my
hero in an incredible week that inspired and spurred
me to move to SIngapore.

Spending time with the amazing animals of Necker Island, including this little guy—a gorgeous lemur who wasn't afraid to get up close and personal!

Celebrating the opening of our first office in Singapore
with a traditional lion dance, September 2016. My
biggest supporters, Charlotte and Amelie, are by
my side.

Charlotte and Amelie welcoming the lion dancers.

Bawah Reserve, Indonesia, June 2017. Reuniting with many of my friends from Necker Island, but on an island closer to Singapore! Those few days of bliss gave me a great dose of inspiration, and kept my entrepreneurial spirit alive.

Launching YoungGems®, Gemstar's programme for young entrepreneurs, in Singapore, October 2018.

Keeping a smile on my face as I proudly open our Innovation Centre in Perth, June 2018.

With Phil Forrest after winning the Entrepreneur
of the Year Award in Singapore, conferred by the
Australian Chamber of Commerce, July 2018.

PART THREE

LIVING A WHOLE LIFE

CHAPTER FIVE
FAMILY

I love our daughters more than anything in the world
—more than life itself. And while that may not be the
first thing some folks want to hear from an Ivy-league-
educated lawyer, it is truly who I am. So for me, being
Mom-In-Chief is, and always will be, job number one.

— Michelle Obama

Being a mother has never been the sole identity defining me. I was not the little girl who played with baby dolls dreaming of a future where I would become an actual mother myself. My career, and my own hopes and dreams, are just as important to me.

But I'm also not the type to outsource my role as a parent. I was never going to put the girls in childcare just so I could spend long hours in the office working away from them. My girls have been integrated into my business from day one. I've brought them to my meetings and the office, and they know the business better than nearly anyone else.

They even understand the mechanics of business, which I find incredible. It surprised even myself how devoted and willing I was and still am, to my daughters' growth. When we first moved to Singapore, with mounting bills and being short on resources, the girls were home-schooled—we had to juggle distance education and business problems. We did without a helper, unlike most expatriate families. I'm still the one sending my daughters to school each morning, and then spending time with them in the evening. I don't take shortcuts!

My mission for carving out a better path for them kicked in because of the circumstances surrounding Charlotte's birth. Being treated as if I was less than capable just because I was birthing another human being felt like a slap in the face. And I never want my daughters or any other woman to face such unfair treatment. That is why I'm so passionate about the work I do, and why it is so important to me.

It is strange how things have turned out. Neither pregnancy was planned in advance, although I did know during that time in life that I wanted children. And I did not expect to mirror Mum's path either; a strong woman raising two girls by herself while working hard to survive. I'm from a long lineage of strong and independent women, so this really shouldn't have been a surprise. I've my gorgeous Mum to thank for all her strength and grace, and the hard work and dedication she has demonstrated and modelled for my sister and me over the years. She is a pillar of strength. She is beautiful inside and out. She was there at each of the natural births of my daughters, literally greeting and welcoming them into the world. And to this day, even though we live in different parts of the world, the four of us (Mum, the girls and I) are a very tight, close unit. Our bond is like no other.

NATURAL BIRTHS

I can't seem to escape my dogged determination! You just need to look at the births of my two girls. When I became pregnant with Charlotte, around this time I was asked to be the birth support person for the birth of my dear friend Gemma's first son. I was so honoured to be asked to play this role by Gemma, and it was a beautiful experience. To see her birth her son, and watch a new human being literally enter the world, was incredible.

My pheromones must have been working a treat though, and sure enough, Charlotte was due nine months after the birth of my friend's son. I was inspired by my friend to have a natural birth—she had made it look so easy!

So, despite some murmurings by those around me about choosing a natural birth, I wasn't going to let anything deter me. I put my mind to having a natural birth with Charlotte, and I wanted my own mother at the birth too, to welcome her as she arrived.

It was so amazing to birth a baby into the world like that, fully present and engaged. The human body is such a wonder, and to be able to do this was a great privilege. Charlotte's birth was a relatively straightforward process, but afterwards I lost a lot of blood and needed a transfusion.

But despite being knocked around by the transfusion, when it came to Amelie's arrival, I was determined once again to give birth in the same birthing centre. Mum was there again (along with Tristan) for Amelie's arrival—my little lioness, who shares her birthday with Madonna.

Speaking of the meaning behind numbers and birthdates, Charlotte arrived in the world the day after my dad's birthday, and Amelie less than a week after my mum's!

WORKING MUM JUGGLE

I've never had the luxury of not working, and my daughters are fully aware of that. My girls have always been around business, and they understand things that I don't think other children totally get at that age. It's the result of growing up around adults and having engaging conversations with people who don't talk down to them, who instead talk to them. My girls get so much from this. They are really interested in things beyond their age.

That doesn't mean they have been robbed of their childhood. On the contrary, I've always encouraged them to play and be creative, and showered them with love and warmth. Amelie, my 11-year-old, still loves to role-play, whether it is pretending to be a shopkeeper, teacher, film director, comedian, lawyer or talk show host. I encourage my girls to be children, and not to grow up too quickly. At the same time, I don't shelter them from the world. Our move to Singapore, and the circumstances around it and our journey together, has been like the school of life for them.

The girls have attended almost all of the major events of our business—whether it was our programmes to Singapore when we were still living in Sydney, Manning & Co.'s fifth anniversary party, the opening of the Singapore and Perth offices, or the graduation event for our YoungGems® programme with the deaf and hard of hearing. They are the best helpers! They help with events by greeting guests, ticking off their names on the guest list, providing name tags, giving the goodie bags out and socialising with guests.

They've done this since they were knee-high, and aren't your average young girls. At one event, they confidently struck up a conversation with one of our good friends and supporters, Chief Scientist Peter Klinken of the Western Australian government. "I've heard so much about the both of you!" he said. "Do you know what my job is?"

Amelie replied, "Yes, you look at science, and you look at policies, and your work involves the both of them together."

He was impressed, as most people are by how articulate my girls are! Another time when Charlotte was 5, I remember I had to deliver a marketing strategy for one of my Manning & Co. clients and it was during the school holidays. I didn't have care for Charlotte on that day, so I took her with me.

I was presenting a rather detailed and intricate new brand strategy for my client, and right at that moment Charlotte jumped out of her chair, came over and gave me the tightest hug imaginable. I was rather taken aback as Charlotte can be a little bit shy at times, and she did this in front of at least 30 people. She hugged me for the rest of my 30-minute presentation, as I tried to get through presenting new ideas and concepts to the client.

On our way home, when it was just the two of us, I asked her, "Darling, that was a lovely cuddle. What made you get up and give me such tight cuddles at that particular moment?"

"Mummy, I love seeing you do your work and I'm so proud of you," she said. It warmed my heart so much.

There is the debate over whether, as women, we can have it all. And at times I beat myself up and think that I should have spent more time with the girls, or played more with them while they were still babies or toddlers at home. But I believe that I've managed the juggle as well as anyone could. I've given it my all—both motherhood and my work. I still make the girls their lunches, iron their uniforms, read to them at night and help with homework. I'm present as much as I can be.

Yes, there have been moments where I've to negotiate on our time together. For example, during the early weeks of the COVID-19 quarantine period, I had to work from home and Amelie was on her school holidays. I had to explain to her, "Darling, I've got so much going on. I can't take a full day off just because I'm home. It's just not how it works." So instead, I took Amelie out for a few special short outings, so that I was still online as much as possible.

Juggling motherhood and business is exhausting and not easy, I won't lie. But I've always been open with the girls and honest with them about the situation. They know that I am doing the best I can. I really want them to know that they should never have to rely on anybody else for their own livelihoods, or think that after they are married they don't have to work for anything for the rest of their lives. It stems from my own experiences and what I've seen. How scary it is for things to not go to plan, or to have the rug pulled out from under you—like Mum experienced with the aquarium business.

The girls know that I do as much as I can to give them the most fulfilling and enriched childhood. For example, I took Charlotte to Vietnam with me on one business trip to do design and development work with a partner based there who employs people with disabilities. Charlotte was 11 then, and I know it was an experience that she will never forget.

For me, it's just not about being 'book-smart', but equipping them with the survival skills, resourcefulness, mindset and attitude they need—and that we teach in my YoungGems® programme. Books help, but you pick them up by applying them in the real world.

I want them to know and remember that they need to be independent, stand on their own two feet and have a voice at the table. That one can and should dream as big as possible but one also needs to work for that dream. Amelie shares her birthday with Madonna, and need I say more? She wants to be a triple threat—a comedian, businesswoman and actor. As her mother, I know she'll do big things in the future. She's got the greatest sense of comedic timing even for a 11-year-old, and had the audience eating out of her hand when she emceed my fortieth birthday celebration.

I don't ever squash my daughters' dreams, but I do remind them that achieving them will take hard work. "If you want that mansion in New York one day, you have to work for it," I tell them.

In both parenting and leading at work, I tend to wear my heart on my sleeve, and I'm not good at hiding my feelings. But there is strength in that. My caring personality, and my genuine desire to have a positive impact on the world, have also rubbed off on my daughters. I can see that they are going to be kind, caring, thoughtful, independent women when they grow up.

Charlotte, for example, is really interested in becoming a human rights lawyer. She turns 14 at the end of 2020 and as she gets older, her interest in this area is really firming up. She cares a lot about women's rights and giving back to society. Perhaps she's learnt from this quality of mine—when I was in school, I was friends with a wheelchair-bound girl with cerebral palsy.

None of the other girls in my class wanted to talk to her, simply because she had a disability. I could not believe that nobody wanted to be friends with her, and so I became her only friend in school.

She was incredibly intelligent, and it was apparent back then too. I would look after her at every class, and just give her my time. I took her on outings after we finished high school, and she even visited Japan! She has a wicked sense of humour too. We still keep in touch today, and she is now an incredible lawyer.

She continues to do so well, even with all these difficult challenges stacked up against her. I've the utmost respect for her, and it really angers me when people pick on others just because they are not 'normal'.

LEAD FIRMLY BUT GENTLY

My mother was strict in her parenting, while still being liberal. This just means that she stated the boundaries very clearly while allowing us the freedom to lead our lives within them. Mum was constantly working to ensure that we had a roof over our heads and food on the table, so she could not be the kind of parent who would hover over our shoulders making sure that we did our homework.

That is what I admire and emulate from her parenting style. That freedom within boundaries allowed me to grow and flourish. I knew my responsibilities, and I could make my own decisions. A growing child needs to learn what's right and what's wrong, while the parent is there to guide and pick them up if they need it. That doesn't mean that my daughters are perfect little angels. When it comes to discipline, they know when they have crossed the line and when to apologise. The worst threat would be having to tell Nanny (my mother) about their naughty behaviour!

I don't agree with helicopter parenting, or micro-managing my children's lives. I believe in having a strong, supportive, and loving environment while allowing them to make their own mistakes and to grow and learn from them. To create an entrepreneurial community or a nation, where skills in problem-solving, creativity, and innovation can be developed and harnessed, it starts when children are young. If parents were to do everything for their children, how can they think outside of the box? How can they dare to think on their feet?

I trust my daughters, and I've to trust that they will do the right thing. My main job is to be very clear on what the boundaries are. But I also allow them the wiggle room within those boundaries to discover things for themselves and learn from their own mistakes. I get cross with them, but I don't tell them they are wrong, nor do I discourage them. I facilitate their thinking through the issue in a respectful way.

When I saw Michelle Obama speak, I thought, "My God, I really connect with this woman and her parenting style!" Because she has the same view as I do—that of teaching kindness and demonstrating respect. It's not about having your children think that you know it all and therefore they must listen to you. It's about letting them have a voice at the table, while conveying their thoughts in a respectful way.

In Singapore, I tend to see a trend in behaviour within the entrepreneurship sphere. When the going gets tough, it is almost too easy to give it all up. This is what happens when you don't allow your child to fall over, or go out in the rain, or eat dirt. Keeping them in a bubble when they are young will make them fear failure too much to dare to do anything.

It all really begins at home. How you parent, and the kind of values you model and teach, will have a huge impact on how our own society will grow, evolve, and ultimately (I hope) thrive in an ever-changing world.

CHAPTER FIVE
A WOMAN IN BUSINESS

> Treating people with kindness and respect seems
> elementary but is not always reciprocated. I often
> run into people who tell me a story about how
> I impacted their life—most often by an act of
> kindness that they never forgot.
>
> — April Uchitel

Always keep your wits about you. I saw what can happen first-hand to women in a business setting in 2012, when I found myself in the remote historic gold-mining town of Kalgoorlie. It's in the Goldfields-Esperance region of Western Australia, some 600 km approximately east of Perth. It sits right at the end of the Great Eastern Highway.

Kalgoorlie was a fitting site for Australia's largest mining conference. It was known internationally as *the* conference to attend for deals between miners and investors. I was there supporting the release of a client's thought leadership report, and it was my first time in Western Australia.

It struck me how few women there were—just 300 out of some 2,500 participants. You can imagine how females stood out, and I remember how uncomfortable I felt on the flight in, as the only woman among 400 men. It wasn't the first time that I'd felt like a fish out of water, but certainly an experience that I will never forget.

Upon arriving in Kalgoorlie, it didn't take long to work out that this wasn't your normal kind of conference. On the very first evening, we who had made the long journey from Sydney headed straight out for dinner at one of the two main pubs.

Little did I know that it wasn't your typical type of country pub. My client threw the door open, and I was greeted by what the conference called 'skympies'—topless female entertainers, specially brought in from Sydney and the Gold Coast!

My initial awkwardness turned to outright discomfort as I realised that I was expected to talk business, meet journalists and set up initial briefings, *all* while being served by nearly-nude women! It certainly shocked me, but the conference regulars found it completely normal.

My initial shock didn't end there. The following day, among conference goings-on and arranging interviews for my client with both broadcast and print media, both of us were invited to a lunch. I was excited to get the invite, as there were some key influential people attending, and I thought it would be great networking for my client.

I was seated near the head of the table next to one such influencer whom we greatly wanted to meet. I hoped to pitch my client's report and see if I could secure a speaking opportunity for us. We had a pleasant lunch, and as we were preparing to leave, this man leant across to me and whispered, "Gemma, I will be waiting for you tonight at The Palace. You might want to cross your legs though when you are at the bar, as I will be eagerly waiting!"

I was absolutely speechless—had a highly-ranked, influential man just propositioned me so boldly, grotesquely and openly at a business lunch? I definitely stayed clear of that place that evening!

At first, I thought my experience in Kalgoorlie was rather extreme. However, I've since spoken to many women who have had similar experiences, and found such behaviour to be sadly common—both in remote locations like Kalgoorlie and in big cities.

I had had another frightening and illustrative experience before, though not from a potential business collaborator. At 23, I was in Philadelphia for a global sales conference—it was my first time in the US, and I was excited but also anxious about travelling by myself. My colleagues arrived a couple of days after me, so I was on my own initially.

While I was waiting for my luggage, I had a man on my flight come up to me, nosily asking why I was there and where I was staying. He tried to get my business card from me, and gave me his own when

I declined. He then followed me to the taxi line. That same trip, my colleagues and I were having a drink at the bar following our first day at the conference, and we met another group of people who were in the healthcare sector too, and related to the company I was working for at the time.

Later that night when I was back in my room getting ready for bed, one of the men from that other group called my room telephone and invited me to come back downstairs. I said no, but he called again and again. I ignored all his calls, but a few minutes later I saw the shadow of feet in the crack under my door. This man stood there for what seemed like an eternity, and I was so terrified I called security. I was so petrified that it took me forever to roll over to the phone.

I've always travelled for my work, since an incredibly young age. I would be lying if I said I didn't often feel vulnerable. Even now, I'm very mindful for when I travel for business, and always have my wits about me. Women travelling on their own can definitely be targets, and the need to be mindful and know the right tactics to deal with such situations is an unfortunate reality of life.

NICE GIRLS DO WIN IN THE END

We have heard of the book and the idea that b*tches get the corner office and nice girls tend to finish last. But I achieved that while only 25, and remaining the person that I am. I've had a ton of amazing experiences, from meeting incredible people in Antarctica and Necker Island, to travelling all over the world for my career.

I chalk it all up to hard work. I certainly did not have to step all over another person to get to where I am now. And I did it on my own merits, despite the deliberate obstacles that were put in my way just because of my gender, and at times my age.

I've often questioned how I could get any rewards for being ethical, when this world of business is so notorious for dirty dealings and shameful behaviour. The answer is that I approach everything

I do in my work with the main principle of doing the right thing. In this trying period, I must make difficult decisions. Yes, it is my own livelihood at stake, but I also feel a great responsibility to my team. As their leader, I must keep going even when the world is behaving less than nobly.

As I keep doing the right thing in business, have I lost out in any way? If I had been a bit more ballsy, more of a hard ass, could my business have gone further? Would I have been able to avoid some of the problems I've encountered? Could I have been able to charge more in this or that deal?

I don't know. But I do know I can't be someone I'm not. I'm *This Girl*, and those who meet me are pleasantly surprised to have found someone who is authentic and the real deal, because there are so many two-faced, deceitful people out there. But this is just the way I am—without a good head on my shoulders for business, I wouldn't have been doing this for this long. But I do wonder sometimes if I've undersold or undercharged. This is why I've the right staff now to delegate those negotiations to. Stay nice and stay ethical, but don't let anyone else take advantage of you.

MENTORS

I'm dedicated to gender equality, because I know first-hand how the glass ceiling impedes and frustrates our efforts to move forward. I've encountered sexist men in the work setting, but have also met men who saw my potential and wanted me to succeed. I've even met young men who recognised the toxic male-dominated culture, and thus were intent on changing their own future work environments.

In fact, I've several more male than female mentors, most of them accomplished businessmen who have taken me under their wing. For example, my non-executive director here in Singapore, Phil Forrest, is like a rock star in Singapore's business community. He's become more than a mentor over the years, and is now a solid friend to me.

When I first came into Singapore, a lot of people questioned how long I would survive. In my experience, the Australian business community in Singapore can be very political and competitive, and it is something I've struggled with at times. So the fact that Phil believed in me right from the start has been an oasis in a hostile environment. At times, just having his name associated with me in business also sends the message that I'm to be taken seriously. Having his support has been invaluable.

Yes, I'm kind, generous and loving, and I lead with my heart, but I'm also a serious businesswoman. If you are going to discount me, you have got something coming because I'm not just going to give up or fade away. My mentors around me know that I'm a force to be reckoned with, and thus support me.

Peter Klinken, the Chief Scientist of the state of Western Australia, is another mentor of mine. I've described in earlier chapters the difficulties of getting into WA and Perth in particular—it was like the Wild West, where people were trying to muscle us out before we even opened. So the Peter Klinkens of the world, who want to see me succeed, help. When I was doing an event for our deaf and hard-of-hearing community, having him just be in the room showed that I'm a serious and credible player in the field.

I did not seek these mentors out myself; they saw the potential and determination in me and so they lent their support. So many people in this world want a quick fix, the shortcut to fame and the billionaire fund line. But I don't want handouts or financial support—as a woman in business, I simply want a level playing field, and to be treated the same, paid the same and commanding the same fees as my male counterparts. I may be a pleasant and petite woman, but that should not be a disadvantage to me, or to anyone else.

MAKING A DIFFERENCE

Back in 2016 on Necker Island, I pitched my Light Years project to Sir Richard Branson, and he saw its potential immediately. He and I come from similar schools of thought in that there is power in entrepreneurship to make a difference in society, and one doesn't need to go to university to acquire those skills. Skills like being courageous and bold, taking calculated risks and having a firm belief in yourself are all part of a constant learning journey that we impart through our programmes aimed at giving back to society.

Light Years focuses on the women categorised as NEETs—that is, Not in Education, Employment, or Training. They are usually youths between the ages of 16 and 24, though I would like to further extend this group to include older women, as many have lives impacted by domestic violence and divorce. As I write, what I've started through YoungGems® and HiddenGems is now being extended to the migrant community in Australia.

Branson is on board with the power of entrepreneurship (and entrepreneurship education) to uplift women around the world. Think about the hundreds of thousands of women classified as NEETs. Many of them have given up their dreams because they married young, or have had their lives negatively impacted because of abusive partners, and so on. If you lifted all these people up, the economic benefit to their countries would be incredible! It will change an entire future generation. I think that is what excited him and others about Light Years.

Ours isn't the only such programme, but ours does take a more holistic view in trying to break this cycle. Other programmes work on providing grants, rewriting CVs and providing recycled corporate wear—all valuable efforts, but not addressing the long-term issues behind women's situations. The gamechanger is in knowing that we need to create independent, resourceful women. That's the core issue, and if we don't address it, everything else is just a temporary band-aid.

We've a generation to help out of this stuck space, and any holistic solution will need a community to dream up and put into action. Light Years thus will teach entrepreneurship skills while also supporting and nurturing confidence. Another arm to it is job creation, because the idea is to close the loop by being able to transition participants into a pathway with a career. That is what we have been experimenting with through our YoungGems® programme, which is offered to all sorts of people from different walks of life.

It is amazing when you truly and properly listen to somebody. The programme may teach the entrepreneurship skills needed, but it also provides empathy, care and genuine nurture. It's giving them the space to flourish, where before they have been excluded just because they don't fit the 'right' mould. That's why our 10 deaf people in HiddenGems credit it for changing their lives—it's in the delivery, the care we take, and the authenticity. I think that can be scaled up... and taken far and wide.

These things never happen overnight, so for me building up our businesses in Manning & Co. and Gemstar has also gotten us a bit closer to the realisation of Light Years. I'm looking for partners to be able to do this as a non-profit. And to find those partners, I need to walk the talk more in the business world, to show that I do have the right experience to carry this through.

After Necker Island, I've had a few conversations with Virgin Unite, the social impact arm of Branson's empire. The idea was for them to be a corporate partner to Light Years. When I first pitched to him, I did not have an educational platform yet, and so I had to build these foundations myself. One big thing I've learnt from my conversations with him is that he appreciates seeing progress in people. It's not about sitting around waiting for him to swoop in with the monetary help. Some people probably think they will get a shortcut with high-net worth people but when I went to Necker, my aim was not to get funded. It was more about the experience of being connected and then having his support from afar, which to me carries far more weight.

I think it is important to remember that your network will serve you very well if you deal with it in an authentic way, not by using others, but caring for them and helping people who'll help you back. It takes time to build, and you must do your utmost to protect its integrity.

MY LIFE TODAY

2020 brought with it the COVID-19 crisis, a very trying time for me. I was very close to packing it all up and going home. I called my mum, and she told me to think it through. Did I really want a tiny virus to cause me to give up my stay in Singapore?

I eventually realised that I'm not done with this adventure yet. My own daughters echoed these sentiments. During our early years in Singapore, grappling with their homesickness and their adjusting to a new environment, my girls at times expressed how much they missed home and their family. But this time they were firm in their decision. "It isn't the time yet, Mummy," they said. And I concurred.

It is in times of real self-doubt like these that I question myself incessantly. The old doubts still come back to the surface—*who the hell am I kidding? I'm not a superwoman, maybe I've been deluding myself?*

During this particularly trying period, I've felt deflated and defeated. But I know that if I had gone home then, I would not be able to rebuild things in Singapore all over again. I'm where I am, and it's here that I'll keep bouncing back and reinforcing a positive message. All of us know that I don't give up—the secret sauce is resilience and dogged determination through the pits of hell, because I know it is not over yet.

To my surprise, a few weeks later after this internal turmoil, new work came in and I achieved more of my business goals. We've navigated through one of the toughest times in history for businesses, and I have dedication, determination and resilience to thank for that.

IN THE MEDIA

Entrepreneur has Branson's ear on jobs

Sydney entrepreneur Gemma Manning is set to pitch a business idea to Richard Branson aimed at helping disadvantaged women.

UPDATED 13/05/2016   SHARE  

Entrepreneur Gemma Manning is jetting off to pitch her business idea to billionaire Richard Branson in a bid to create thousands of jobs for disadvantaged women.

Ms Manning, the founder of two Sydney-based businesses, will have the ear of Mr Branson next week on his private tropical island, where he is hosting an event for entrepreneurs.

"I'm quite nervous, a little bit on edge," Ms Manning told AAP.

"The project is pretty special to me."

The mother of two girls will seek support for her venture Light Years, a program which aims to help 18 to 25 year-old disadvantaged women excel in work and life.

"I feel quite passionate that I want my own girls to grow up in a world where it doesn't matter what background you're from, whether you're female or male, you should be able to follow your dreams and have an equal opportunity," she said.

Light Years plans to recruit women who are not in employment, education or training, and offer online education, mentoring, coaching, workshops and holistic development.

Ms Manning said she is determined to make the project happen and will accept any assistance from Mr Branson and his Virgin businesses.

The Light Years business plan, which has been three years in the making, has aims of creating at least 2000 jobs and potentially thousands more globally.

"This is a project that has global application and hopefully social and economic impacts around the world," she said.

"Having been a businesswoman experiencing a number of challenges myself first hand, coming from an educated background and a middle class upbringing, I can't imagine some of the challenges that young women have that haven't been as fortunate as me."

SBS News
https://bit.ly/3IznRW0

CAREER NEWS TRENDS

Businesswoman Gemma Manning's Amazing Advice To Entrepreneurs

 by **Sneha Khale** · 2 years ago

Just last week, Australian businesswoman Gemma Manning, founder and Managing Director of strategic marketing consultancy firm Manning and Co (M&C), and international accelerator Gemstar, was awarded the Australia Chamber of Commerce Singapore's Entrepreneur of the Year Award.

The award coincided with the announcement of the Gemstar Singapore team launching a *Diploma in Entrepreneurship and Innovation* with private education institute Kaplan later this year, as well as the opening of the Gemstar Innovation Centre in Perth which opens next week. In a sit-down interview with Sneha Khale, managing editor o*Women Love Tech*, Gemma talked about her businesses and their expansion across the Asian market, her move to Singapore from Australia and its challenges and rewards, being a female entrepreneur and a role model to her daughters, finding stimulating causes to work for, and pitching to Sir Richard Branson!

Womenlovetech
https://bit.ly/35xrKFi

EPILOGUE
A PURPOSEFUL LIFE

> Fight for the things you care about, but do it in a way
> that will lead others to join you.
>
> — Ruth Bader Ginsburg

Even if it all went pear-shaped tomorrow, I think I could say, with hand on heart, that I've built some amazing things from scratch. These are Manning & Co., Gemstar and my YoungGems® programmes, and next Light Years. I've built all of these ventures from nothing and grown them in promising markets. I might not be a billionaire, and I probably will not have a private island and all those other trappings of success, because for me money is not a measure of success.

I'm driven by a sense of achievement, and I gain fulfilment when I see my goals through. To be building my business across Australia and Asia is no mean feat, even if it is a comparatively small one. I think we tend to get caught up in measuring success by comparing with others, and by trying to put numbers to things. But what I essentially look for in where I am and what I've achieved is whether I'm truly happy.

I still have a long way to go. My form of success will blossom when I've launched Light Years and through it helped thousands of women around the world; when I've empowered more deaf and hard-of-hearing people through my HiddenGems programme; when I've taken YoungGems® digitally to places that I can't physically get to. And doing all of that, perhaps I will eventually sell Manning & Co., or another business that I've created

I'm also deeply passionate about the Australia-Singapore (and Asia more broadly) business relationship. There is a lot of lip service paid to untapping Asia's potential by Australian businesses. However, I've seen that a lot of Australian businesses don't have experience with Asia, or don't place people with experience in Asia on their boards. In the future, I would like to continue to advise Australian businesses in how to do business here. There are cultural aspects that need to be navigated carefully, requiring cultural intelligence and respect for our host countries on our parts. Sometimes Australian companies get it wrong when there is an arrogance of not wanting to adapt or show respect. Maybe that is why I'm still here, still able to do business—because I'm respectful. When I lived in Japan, I spoke Japanese the whole time, because I adapted to their culture.

My mentor Phil Forrest has done incredibly well in Singapore because he doesn't push the Australian way of doing things. Because he is very respectful, he is in turn respected in the Singapore business community, especially since he has given back immensely to Singapore. He is in the Singapore Institute of Company Directors, and he really pushes gender diversity here too. I look at why he is a success here, and understand that those things are important. This is what I would like to impart to other businesses coming here in the future.

MY ROLE MODELS

I respect and look up to Sir Richard Branson not because he is a billionaire, but because of his values and ethics. He's self-made, disrupting the big players, shaking down industries and even having governments against him. When I've had difficulties, I've often wondered, "Far out. Why is the government doing this to us? Why would they not want to see businesses do well? Why do corporates want to crush potential collaborative partners?" I'm just a small player, and that's why I look up to Branson being the David against so many Goliaths.

Other people I look up to are former US First Lady Michelle Obama and actress Reese Witherspoon to name but a few, but also my dear entrepreneurial friends—Ginger Jones (who kindly wrote the Foreword) and Amanda Fry are two that come to mind. I love Obama for how she carries herself, her strength and her lovely way of being authentic and being able to connect with others despite her position as First Lady. Her determination and how she raises her girls are so admirable as well.

Witherspoon was also discounted early on in her career for being a young blonde, and stereotyped into the roles she acted in. But despite that she turned out to be an amazing businesswoman who paved the way for other women in the industry through her production company, by producing films centred on women and giving more actresses starring roles. That needs to be commended. Another role model is Kylie Minogue, and my thoughts on her achievements have been mentioned extensively at the beginning of this book. And of course all of the women in my family who have come before me—that goes without saying.

I truly identify with strong women, those who are passionate and live life with purpose—and who aren't afraid to go out and make a change, to shake things up in this world.

LOOKING BACK

I don't live a life filled with regrets and what-ifs. I've taken some gigantic risks in my life, both personally and professionally, and I'm glad I made them because I'm not left wondering "what if?" I've learnt that it is ok to lead with your heart, even if it doesn't always work out. Leading with your heart can be a risk, both personally and professionally, but that is a risk that I'm willing to take. Being passionate about what you do and having something to stand for is important.

I'm not perfect by any means, but I'm proud to say that I've lived my life thus far being true to my core values—and living an authentic life. And I want my girls to be able to do the same with their lives too.

People may not agree or may not understand the decisions you make, or the life choices you choose to take. There have been some very ugly times and no doubt people around me at different times have had their own views on events as they have unfolded. When I went through my separation, I was surprised by the fact that I lost friends who could not walk that path with me for their own reasons.

But these twists and turns are ever present in any path. I trust my gut, and so I trust that sometimes the path I'm on might force me to places that are difficult to go through. It helps to have that sense of intuition, because even when I know it is hard, I've faith that I'm on the right path. It takes courage and bravery to live life like this.

I became a bit more spiritual when I turned 32. This was during the height of my personal turmoil, when I had so many questions over everything that was happening. I had never sought clarity from anyone else, and my own trusted family doctor instructed me, "Gemma, you have a lot going on. I think you should go and talk to someone." At that same time, my mum had lost her business, and had to sell her home. She was living at times with my sister, and other times with me. That was also the first time I was living without Tristan, and we had been together since I was 17. I had found myself no longer having someone that close on my side. Adjusting to life as a single mother after never having experienced singlehood before was another steep learning curve. On top of that, Mum was also battling some health concerns, I was faced with a number of health challenges for one of my daughters, and I was found to have pre-cervical cancer. On and on, everything piled.

I desperately needed some healing to get through what was otherwise a traumatic time in many ways. So my good friend Gemma recommended an energetic healer, who helped me find the clarity I needed. It was an incredibly healing and comforting experience for me, and I've gone to see her many times thereafter—I still see her whenever I'm home in Australia. Through working with her, I found the tools that helped me out whenever I was at the crossroads. Just tapping into my gut instinct has helped me think more clearly through whatever conundrum I'm facing.

This is not just a strange silly quirk; I've heard many entrepreneurs who seek support in this way. I think there is space for that. For meditation, and just being a bit zen to be able to work through this chaotic world.

Another person I've to thank for my sanity is my partner, Martin, whom I met six years ago. After going through so many challenges, it is inevitable to be jaded and shut off your emotions. Thankfully, he has helped me to open up my heart with his inner confidence and quiet strength, which balances my zany energy. He is very calm, patient, loving and supportive, as it's not easy to be with someone who owns and is consumed by her business. My life is a roller-coaster ride, and knowing that he's in my corner keeps me from falling off.

Looking back, I am happy that I have shown patience, resilience and sheer determination. We now having thriving businesses in WA and Singapore, two of my expansion markets, despite the hard knocks and dirty antics. By keeping it real, professional, ethical and getting on with the job at hand, we have quietly gone about our work delivering great results and attracting great success. We have prevailed. My message: Rise above the dirty politics, keep focused and don't take your eye off the ball. And remember to believe in yourself and be yourself. Being real and authentic has been and will continue to be my secret weapon, and has helped me build longevity in my business success.

SISTERS ARE DOING IT FOR THEMSELVES

I was extremely fortunate to have grown up with my sister by my side. I look at the close bond my girls have, and it reminds me of my sister and me. When we were younger, my sister and I were inseparable. Always together. We even had our own special sisters club. When we spent time on our boat, Nat would wake me up at midnight and we would go up on the deck with our doonas and torch and get under the covers to discuss all-important "sister business." We even had a special notebook that we would jot our notes down in. I see the same closeness in the girls and they are fiercely protective of each other.

Nat and I have had spurts of living in other countries during our adult years (Nat lived in London when I lived in Japan, and now she is in Sydney while I am in Singapore), but the deep bond and protectiveness is always there. When Nat was in London, I visited her as a 23-year-old and we spent the most amazing time together traveling around Italy, Paris and London. As two young women travelling on our own, we attracted a fair bit of unwanted attention along the way. One time in Florence, we were walking towards the market with my sister slightly in front of me, when a young man ran by and tried to steal my sister's bag. It happened so quickly and before I knew it, I had come up behind him and pushed him to the ground, despite his greater height. No one was going to hurt or steal from my sister!

My sister is the one person who can make me have a big belly laugh, often at the most inappropriate times. Like the time when we were in Italy and we were eating liquorice and then decided to go into a sacred church site where you had to be quiet. Looking over at each other to smile, we noticed that we both had black liquorice all over our teeth. Well, we started giggling uncontrollably and were almost asked to leave. Then there was the time Nat dared me to go into a masquerade store in Venice and pose in the front window, which I did to her surprise and once again we were in stitches.

One of my most favourite things is laughing with my sister. We don't get the chance to do it enough these days, but when we do, it feels so good. I have missed having that while living in Singapore, and I crave it when the going gets tough as it has many times the last few years. Being able to laugh through difficult times is a perfect remedy for stress. There is also something very therapeutic and soothing about a sister—may the girls protect what they have when they are grown up too.

THE FUTURE

I hope to be celebrated as someone who is kind, caring and loving; as someone who has good values and lived a truly authentic life at no matter what risk; who did not allow any setback, personally or in professional life, to keep her from moving forward.

I want to create a more level playing field for future generations. It's not about making it *easier*, but clearer and fairer. If our daughters' paths were a bit more straightforward whether they wanted to be politicians, scientists or actresses, would it not be better?

I want to see a world where they don't have to fight so hard just because of their gender. I want to see a world that can be respectful of the differences everybody has, to demonstrate kindness and be inclusive.

It saddens me when people are shut out from society just because they are different.

The world's cruelty can come in all sorts of different forms. Entrepreneurship, for example, remains male-dominated. More women are founding companies, but the numbers are still skewed—out of every five new start-ups to receive their first funding in 2019, only one was led by a woman.[3] I hope the proportion of female to male entrepreneurs will achieve parity in this lifetime, but it can only be done if there is concerted effort to support it.

In the future, I would like to be more hands-on in driving the YoungGems® programme and Light Years as part of it, as I see women being more vulnerable during these uncertain times.

Regardless, entrepreneurship doesn't have to be something that our children should stumble upon later in life and then blindly crawl their way through. There is power in teaching it to our children from an early age, as it encourages more problem solving and creative thinking away from the conventional rote-learning that most children encounter in schools. It gives them the confidence to take risks, to pick themselves up from their failures, to learn how to press on and when to cut their losses. My own girls are pitching a business idea—a skincare platform for teens, and I plan to back and invest in it. I can't wait to see what they do with it, and to see how they grow their idea into something flourishing.

As I write, we're still in Singapore riding out the COVID-19 crisis with the rest of the world. Despite the difficulties I've encountered since being here, Singapore is home. Singapore is this little red dot, but there's so much more to it than meets the eye. Thinking about the parallels between entrepreneurship and being resilient, creating something from nothing,

---

[3] Gené Teare, "EoY 2019 Diversity Report: 20 Percent Of Newly Funded Startups In 2019 Have A Female Founder," CrunchBase, 21 January 2020, at https://news.crunchbase.com/news/eoy-2019-diversity-report-20-percent-of-newly-funded-startups-in-2019-have-a-female-founder.

Singapore's modern history reflects that very well. What better place to live your entrepreneurial journey and dream, than here on this little (but mighty) red dot?

To further cement my bond, I've recently won the account of an iconic Singaporean brand during this pandemic, which is a huge validation for me. It proves that all my years of hard work is being recognised. I can't help but wonder if this is a signal from the Universe, telling me that my destiny is here.

I can't wait for this next decade, and to see what my journey uncovers next.

A LETTER TO MY DAUGHTERS

To my darlings—Charlotte and Amelie,

The moment each of you entered the world, life became that much more complete and filled with purpose, happiness and joy. You light up my world, and you are my everything.

Given my love of astrology, your birth dates fascinate me. Charlotte, people born on 28 December are often described as "simple sophistication." And Amelie, people born on 16 August are "high voltage"—isn't that the truth? I've always thought that these birth date descriptions sum you both up perfectly!

Charlotte, your innate sense of style, elegance, grace and sophistication has been with you since the day you were born. And Amelie, you came into the world with a wild roar, and beaming smile. You are high-energy, charismatic, full of love, kindness and kisses, and truly magnetic. Sharing Madonna's birthday, you are one-of-a kind. The actress, the comedian, the storyteller—all rolled into one.

Our bond is something that you don't come by every day. What we have is so natural, pure and simply beautiful. The closeness that we share is by far my greatest achievement. I am thankful every day for bringing you both into the world. I'm so fortunate that I met Daddy and that we were able to create such magnificent human beings together. I am happy that I had you in life when I did, and that the three of us have been able to grow together.

You are both a true gift to me and those around you. You are loved by so many. Never forget that! Thank you for being you. And thank you for your unconditional love and support. For every bad day I have had and for every time I have been knocked down, I have just needed to see your beautiful faces and I am okay again. You are my biggest supporters— always in my corner cheering me on. You might not know it, but you have always given me the strength to keep going with this adventure. You are always encouraging me and reminding me why I am on this path.

Sometimes I wonder if our roles have been reversed, and you're the ones raising and comforting me. I always feel a great comfort when I'm in your presence. You already understand so much about your surroundings, but I also know that you will fully understand and appreciate more of the journey when you are older. I am sorry for all the times that I've ever had to leave you and travel for business—be it from Australia or Singapore. I've lost count of the number of times that I have cried in taxis on my way to the airport, feeling so guilty for leaving you.

Every time that I have ever had to leave you, it's always been painful. It never gets easier, and I'll never forget the night before I left for Antarctica. You both cried yourselves to sleep thinking that I would die from being hit by an iceberg like in *Titanic*! I had to comfort you both half the night, and assure you that wouldn't happen and I would be fine.

I remember the safety briefing when I finally got to Punta Arenas in Chile, and being so worried as they went into great detail about all the possible risks we would face once we set foot on Antarctica. What had I done?

It was such a mission to make that final leg to Antarctica too, and there were some nail-biting moments. The bad weather delayed our trip by three days, as we had to wait for a break just to make it to King George Island. On our first attempt, we were just 30 minutes away only for the weather to worsen, and our plane had to turn back. We were all holding our breath when we finally touched down, ever mindful of the dangers of landing on the narrow runway in bad weather. It was nerve-wracking, and the whole time I was thinking of your comments about the *Titanic*!

(Amelie, I'm sorry too for missing your first day of school, and hopefully you'll forgive me one day. I still remember what I had to go through, making that ship-to-shore call to wish you luck from one of the most remote places on the planet!)

A year later, I was about to take off on my adventure to Necker Island, and Amelie, you told me I should bake more and learn how to make cinnamon rolls. You didn't mean to hurt my feelings, but I remember crying and thinking that there is more to life than baking! I was about to present Light Years to Sir Richard Branson himself, and you thought I needed to improve my baking skills—there's nothing more grounding than that.

I'm sorry for all the times I have crumbled in front of you. As much as I have always tried to be strong and keep any challenging or painful moments from you, you both have seen me break down in tears on too many occasions. I always try to keep those moments for my evening shower when I'm in private and can wash the day away—especially if it has been a bad one. But as we know, there is no privacy in our household! Which I love but sometimes, I do wish that I could deal with things on my own without involving both of you. I'm sorry for the occasions you have witnessed my ocean of tears.

I have so much to share with you, and here's just some of it:

- Always love each other like you do now when you are older. You have a special bond, like the one I have with my sister, your Aunty Nat. The love you have for each other is so special—truly deep and magical. You might not always see it like that, but you have a unique bond. You must stick together, and support and protect each other.

- Be your authentic self at all times, and at all costs! Don't feel like you must ever fit in. Stand out from the crowd and be yourselves. You have the most beautiful, unique souls—there is no other Charlotte or Amelie, so embrace who you are, and dare to be different and real. Don't pretend to be someone you are not. Be true to yourself.

- Practice kindness. We don't have enough kindness in this world, and we need more of it! Have a big heart and think of others. Care for and nurture those around you, and accept people for who they are now, not who you want them to be.

- Be grateful for everything you have in this world, as there are so many others who aren't as fortunate as you.

- Lead with your heart; don't be afraid to love big and lead your life with love and warmth. At some stage, we all have our hearts broken, but it is better to love than not to have loved at all.

- Be prepared for hard work. The most successful people tend to have worked hard for their successes. Don't measure success by money. It is about the impact that you make in this lifetime.

- Dream big and have purpose. Have a growth mindset and don't ever say 'I can't'. You can if you set your mind to it. No mountain is too high. If you believe in what you are doing, and back yourself, you will be fine.

- Be bold and take risks. To achieve truly wonderful things, you need to push beyond your comfort zone at times. It can be scary to do this, but it's the only way to learn and truly grow.

- Use your voices and speak up. We can't change the world and make it a better place if we don't speak up and use the voice we have been given. Use it respectfully and authentically.

- Surround yourself with good, like-minded people. Learn quickly to identify and stay clear of naysayers. You want to surround yourself with positive people with good energy who will lift you up, and not pull you down.

- Always remember that the light that shines from within will always be stronger than the light that shines on you. When you are passionate about and love what you do, when it ignites the fire in your belly and your spark, you will be a shining beacon and an unstoppable force. If your light ever diminishes, come back to what makes you happy, and it will flare up again.

- And finally, remember to dance, laugh and have fun. Don't ever lose your wicked sense of humour or laughter. A house filled with your banter and giggling voices is something that always brings so much joy. Don't let anyone take that away—it is too precious.

Girls, remember that I love you to the moon and back... with a big cherry on top!

Love you always,

Mummy xxx

ACKNOWLEDGEMENTS

Writing *About This Girl* has been an empowering and cathartic experience. It has taken me (and some of my family) right back to the beginning to relive key events that have come to shape me and the journey thus far. The process of writing and reliving life's journey has been a mix of wonderment, happiness, pain and relief—quite an emotional ride really!

Writing this book has presented the same fears that I experience every time I push myself out of my comfort zone and take risks. This book is a huge risk, but one that I am willing to take to share my story in the hope that it will have a positive impact. I am putting my story out there to inspire others yet even through the process, I have doubted myself, questioned why I am doing this and at times have had many sleepless nights over the book. But I set myself the goal to do this at the beginning of 2020 and have been determined to see it through for my girls and for the next generation of female *and* male leaders.

At one stage, I thought, who am I kidding? I started writing the book before COVID-19, but then the once in a lifetime pandemic hit and I lost confidence in why I was writing this book. My journey to becoming an international businesswoman seemed pointless when my business initially took a few serious hits as the world outside of Asia started to react to COVID-19. But I am so glad that I pushed through and continued writing, as it was the perfect time to put pen to paper as I turned the business around and continued to grow my business despite the challenging times.

I haven't approached this project wanting to embarrass or disparage anyone. Some names and events haven't been included; however, I have done my best to recount the key events that have shaped me, and that have led me to where I am today.

I wouldn't be writing this without the love and support of so many people—some I would like to acknowledge here.

Firstly, a very big thank you to my darling Mum for her ongoing support, unconditional love and for always encouraging me to fly. Thank you for believing in what I am doing, even with this book, as always.

To my sister, Natalie, thank you for being such a wonderful big sister, and a great Aunty to the girls—and all the belly laughs you have given me along the way to keep it all real.

And Dad, thank you for the gift of writing. You have always been so good with words—I know where I get it from!

Charlotte and Amelie, you are a true gift and my everything. You come from a long lineage of incredible women and I know that you will carry forward this legacy and go on to do equally incredible things by following your passion and purpose.

Martin, what a roller coaster ride! We have crammed so many adventures in including moving to Singapore. Thank you for your ongoing belief and unwavering support for my various pursuits—and there are many! You always have my back and are in my corner. You have never gotten in my way of flying high—instead you lift me up and ensure I take full flight.

A very special thank you to Renee Pullen, one of my oldest and best friends, for your beautiful illustration that has become the cover of this book. You're truly talented. I couldn't think of anything more fitting than having you, my best friend who has known me for almost 30 years, to collaborate with me on this very personal journey. Thank you from the bottom of my heart.

To Ginger Jones, my beautiful friend and fellow businesswoman, thank you for writing the Foreword to *About This Girl*. How fortunate am I to have met you on the magical Necker and shared a truly remarkable experience together? We have laughed and danced on table tops together, had heart-to-hearts and spoken for hours about juggling fast-growing businesses with motherhood and all that comes with it! You are my soul sister and I draw so much inspiration from you—thank you.

Thank you to all the good men in my life who have been instrumental: David Hand, Phil Forrest, Peter Klinken, Rohan Morrison, Chris Dutton, John Pope, Norman Cipriano, to name but a few. And to my former bosses for seeing that something special in me and always supporting and elevating me in the workplace. Whether you know it or not, you all played a role.

Thank you to my team (past and present) for standing behind my vision and taking pride too in your work with the business. A special thank you in particular to Kate Bagnell, for keeping me sane and listening to my downloads every day. You are the ultimate right-hand woman!

And finally, to all my clients—past and current, and partners, thank you so much from my heart for your support and for choosing me and the company I keep to partner with—whether that is Manning & Co., or Gemstar.

Gemma Manning is a serial entrepreneur and recognised business leader who knows how to stay ahead of the game. Over the past 12 years, she has successfully established two businesses with international reach—Manning & Co., a full-service strategic marketing consultancy (2008), and Gemstar Technology, a launch-pad for start-ups and innovators in Singapore and South-East Asia, and entrepreneurship educator (2013).

Gemma launched her first business at the age of 28 drawing on her corporate marketing and communications experience across a diverse range of industries. Since then, Gemma has evolved Manning & Co. to become a full-service strategic marketing consultancy in the region servicing not only companies across ASEAN, but the globe. Services span brand and marketing strategy and implementation, thought leadership, content marketing, media, creative design, digital marketing development and videography. The team is spread across Australia, Singapore and Indonesia.

Gemstar is a personalised international accelerator and entrepreneur educator with Innovation Centres in Singapore and Perth, with more to come. Gemstar's vision is to unearth entrepreneurial talent to build exciting new businesses with global relevancy. Gemstar has launched a Young Entrepreneurs Program, YoungGems®, that guides budding entrepreneurs by addressing the key reasons why most-start-ups fail. Rather than start with the technology and innovation in mind, Gemstar has designed its programme to be marketing-led—an approach that is key to business success because it helps young talent understand the 'why' of doing business and the problem(s) they are trying to solve.

Among Gemma's many accolades, she was awarded the *Entrepreneur of the Year* award from AustCham in Singapore in May 2018. She was shortlisted for the *Telstra Women's Business Awards 2017* in the category of 'Women Doing Business in Asia'. She has previously been nominated and shortlisted for the *Telstra Young Women's Business Award* (2012 and 2011). In May 2016, Gemma was one of 28 entrepreneurs invited to Richard Branson's Necker Island for a week of collaborative brainstorming. Prior to this, in 2015, Gemma was one of 106 entrepreneurs selected for the exclusive 'Fire on Ice' expedition to Antarctica, an entrepreneurial think tank for Australian entrepreneurs.

Gemma is a regular contributor to high-profile publications *The CEO Magazine*, *The Business Woman Media*, *This Woman Can* and *Business Business Business* in areas such as strategic marketing, women leaders, female entrepreneurship, business development, growth into South-East Asia, start-ups, innovation and personal branding. Gemma also frequently speaks at a range of events in the areas of women in business, innovation, marketing and doing business in Asia.

Gemstar's work in Singapore and ASEAN has been featured extensively over the years in a range of publications, as well as mentioned at the highest level by Singapore's Prime Minister, Mr Lee Hsien Loong, at the 2018 ASEAN summit hosted in Sydney.

Other recent awards for Gemma, Gemstar and Manning & Co. include:

July 2020 – ACQ5
Asia — Full Service Strategic Marketing Consultancy
Gamechanger of the Year

June 2020 – Forrester
One of the top 85 channel-focused PR firms in the world

October 2019 – Global 100
Best Marketing and PR Company 2019 (Asia)

July 2019 – ACQ5
Asia — Full Service Strategic Marketing Consultancy
Gamechanger of the Year

May 2019 – APAC Insider
Best Marketing & PR Company, Australia (2019)

June 2018 – Australia Chamber of Commerce Singapore
Entrepreneur of the Year Award
Shortlisted – Telstra Business Woman of the Year, Asia

As a mother of two daughters, Gemma is passionately committed to the empowerment of women and girls, equal access to education and gender parity in the workforce. In August 2017, Gemma was invited to a high-level Women's Dialogue in Singapore with the Australian Minister for Foreign Affairs, The Hon Julie Bishop MP, and Singaporean Second Minister for Foreign Affairs, Josephine Teo, to help further the discussion around gender diversity at a board level.

She calls Singapore home and lives here with her two daughters, Charlotte and Amelie, partner Martin and their two dogs, Teddy and Audrey. Gemma is celebrated for her unique and authentic entrepreneurial style, visionary leadership and business-savvy mind.

ABOUT THE CO-AUTHOR

Boss Of Me is a boutique book-writing agency run by Pearlin Siow that specialises in helping people write as well as publish books. Together with her team of content specialists, it has produced several bestselling biographies for top entrepreneurs and companies in Singapore. Their clients range from billionaires to stay-at-home mothers.

Connect with Pearlin at www.bossofme.sg.

がんばって

Good luck and do your best!